Earth Absolute

Lorand Gaspar

& Other Texts

Lorand Gaspar

Earth Absolute
& Other Texts

TRANSLATED BY

Mary Ann Caws & Nancy Kline

Contra Mundum Press   New York · London · Melbourne

Sol absolu & autres textes © Editions Gallimard, Paris, 1972, et 1982 pour la présente édition. Translation of *Sol absolu & autres textes* © 2015 Mary Ann Caws & Nancy Kline.

First Contra Mundum Press Edition 2015.

All Rights Reserved under International & Pan-American Copyright Conventions.

No part of this book may be reproduced in any form or by any electronic means, including information storage & retrieval systems, without permission in writing from the publisher, except by a reviewer who may quote brief passages in a review.

Library of Congress Cataloguing-in-Publication Data

Gaspar, Lorand, 1925–
[Sol absolu & autres textes. English.]
Sol absolu & autres textes / Lorand Gaspar; translated from the original French by Mary Ann Caws & Nancy Kline

—1st Contra Mundum Press Edition
272 pp., 5 x 8 in.

ISBN 9781940625126

I. Gaspar, Lorand.
II. Title.
III. Caws, Mary Ann.
IV. Kline, Nancy.
V. Translators & editors.

2015945561

Contents

0   Mary Ann Caws, Preface

VI   Nancy Kline, Introduction

Earth Absolute

2   "They tell me I was born in 1925…" *

26   Approach of the Word

38   The Fourth State of Matter
        Knowledge of the Light
        Iconostasis
        Shells
        The Garden of Stones

94   Earth Absolute *

214   Corrosive Body

230   Bibliography

* Translated by Nancy Kline. All other texts translated by Mary Ann Caws.

Preface

LORAND GASPAR

When I first knew Lorand Gaspar, many years ago in 1982 — though in no way does it feel so long ago —, it was as a poet, a friend of my great poet friend René Char, arriving in New York for the first time. Immediately, he and his wife Jacqueline became great companions and companion walkers around the city, both in Manhattan & in Brooklyn.

 We talked about everything under the sun, it seemed to me, and most particularly, about the lamentable state of bookstores and the possibilities of finding the poets you cared to read, as well as the state of the universe, in its lamentable and yet miracle-worthy being. Being, that's what it was and is about. *Le merveilleux* — roughly speaking, the marvelous, but of course that translation, as it happens with so many renderings of an in-itself marvelous French word, falls far short of what the term meant — & what we meant in speaking together of all this — in the original. We were trying, all three of us, to locate exactly what, in France, in New York, in the world and its political self, was at that moment important to talk about. And, if it isn't too preposterous a thought, I think we were not far from whatever any of us might have conceived as the truth. Then, if you like, and on.

And so we walked and walked, the three of us. And talked and talked. About what mattered, if that's the way to put it, and also what didn't. What did was poetry, in all the senses of that wonderful word. Lorand Gaspar was, in my view, and remains always, a superb embodiment of a poet at that term's best. He had the essential wide-ranging curiosity and knowledge, of people and situations, and shared it willingly.

As both surgeon and poet, manifesting both a scientific and a lyrical mind and expression, he was at that point, for his work, based in Tunisia. Would I come over, he asked, and speak about poetry there? How could I have refused, as I did, in a peculiar timidity I now marvel at? and regret, ah so deeply.

But that could not have mattered in itself: he had and has the generosity of a gentleman intellectual, and remained faithful to ongoing friendship. At that first moment of walking, he had published a first state of *Le Quatrième Etat de la matière*, and offered it to me, as he did all his ensuing works. It wasn't that I could possibly understand the scientific reach of his mind and writing, but that, in his affection, he wanted to give me what he had, and he did.

I wasn't up to the scientific side, but he knew that and pardoned it of course, as he pardoned my eventual never making the voyage he invited me to make. It wasn't that that mattered, it was friendship, the kind of friendship poets can offer and we can accept with our entire selves, wherever we are.

PREFACE

So I was not here when I received my copy of the book we are now publishing with such joy. His inscription in my copy of this *Sol absolu*, or *Earth Absolute*, the work Nancy Kline and I have translated, reads like this, and remains as witness to the voyage I did not make:

> Yesterday in New York was lonely (as are the skyscrapers) without you, but until soon, and in Sidi Bon Said — affectionately, Lorand
>
> Paris March the 1st 1982

But last year I went again to Paris to see Lorand and Jacqueline, and that voyage remains fixed, as an unmistakably poetic moment, in my mind.

> Mary Ann Caws
> New York, May 21, 2014

P.S. One other thing about Lorand Gaspar that may not have appeared in all our translations is his enormous sense of humor along with his no less enormous sense of melancholy — which makes it all the more appropriate that he should have been the winner in 1967 of the Prix Guillaume Apollinaire for his *Fourth State of Matter* — both of them arriving in Paris from somewhere else, & merging a sense of otherness with a particular intimacy with the French language.

Translator's Introduction

In his uprootedness and multiplicity, his life "of movement through space-time, but also… over cognitive and cultural expanses," as he himself has put it (LM 2), Lorand Gaspar mirrors the century of upheavals into which he was born: in 1925, in Transylvania (now part of Romania), into a Hungarian family. He grew up speaking Hungarian, Romanian, and German and, once he entered school, French, the language in which he ultimately chose to live his life and write his poetry. As a very young man, took his "first 'great journey,' if independent of my will" (LM 2), in a closed cattle car, to a German POW camp in Germany. In 1945, he made his way across a world in ruins to Paris, where he studied medicine and 'mutated' into a French citizen (LM 3). It was in 1954 that he became a surgeon at the French hospital in Jerusalem, where he remained for the next sixteen years.

Earth Absolute' is the poet's compendium and distillation of those years in the Middle East, first written as he was preparing to move on again, about to leave this region that he loved but whose turbulence had finally become too disruptive. The text is his long love poem to

> *the' naked song of the Judean mountains which revealed itself to my thirst on the pathways*
> *of Rock-strewn Arabia, desolate and blessed.* (EA 2)

Even this brief dedicatory sentence shimmers with a number of *Earth Absolute*'s major leitmotifs: the poet's thirst, the music of the desolate landscape, the multiple pathways through it, and the epiphanies it offers, the ubiquity of rock. The text brims with light and mystery *&* science, brief lyrics interspersed with longer poems, biblical citations, and prose passages that speak of ancient history, medicine, geology, geography, religion, archeology, linguistics, botany, the act of love, the act of writing, the vigilance required to make poems. In a multiplicity of voices, *Earth Absolute* evokes the desert and the creatures who inhabit it: nomads, saints, burrowing toads, gerbils ("athlete[s] of hydric asceticism" [38]). "ON THE BURNING ROADS ... WITHIN SIGHT OF NOTHING" (6), in "familiarity with the void" (7), these wanderers and isolates (but *are* they isolated, traveling on what Gaspar calls "the unmapped roads of solidarity in motion" [11]?) — these wanderers are joined on the white expanse of the page by the poet, in mid-stride, *"space flung negligently over one shoulder"* (EA 48).

Gaspar tells us in the short autobiographical essay that introduces *Earth Absolute* how, on his first trip to Jerusalem, flying over the desert for the first time, he can't keep his eyes away from *"the rhythmic beige and brown of the great sensual undulations that were' the' mountains of Ammon and Moab."* Instantly seduced, the poet, this *"offspring of a country of forests,"* wonders

INTRODUCTION

> *what was there in my make-up that resonated so immediately with the vibration of this desolate land? In the course of the years, each time I came back to it, after a longer or shorter absence, the perception of these meager colors, these curvatures, these mesas, these rhythmic faults, unfolding as would a fugue, flooded me, physically, with the same simple and unutterable joy… I was in love with this country.* (8–9)

The poet-lover rejoices here, as in *Earth Absolute*, in the land's rich 'meagerness,' and he experiences the body of the desert, its beige curves, its "shimmering pelt" (EA 60) and hidden liquids, not only as a locus of desire but also synesthetically, as a fugue, a grand rhythmic piece of music. He will transcribe this music not just in his choice of words, but also in his idiosyncratic placement of words on the page.

On first reading *Earth Absolute*, one is immediately struck by its typography, which, as Jérôme Hennebert has written, breaks "the linearity of poetic *discourse*" (JH 1) and "spatializes" (JH 2) Gaspar's poetry, as in the following text:

desert

    what remains of music
    when the design is no longer visible
    as if light had eroded
    the time and the place that belong to things
    as if the grammar of the depths were readable
    by the hand illuminated on the regs

anchorites

    lizards

        snakes

            hyenas & cynhyenes

    through the morning's gorges
    on the evening's slopes

the unmapped roads of solidarity in motion

    the wild oryx
    the Arabian gazelle

the wind across the plains of Sam south of the Euphrates

    barillas
    shrivelled shrubs
    sandstone plateaus
    sheer-cut psammites
    streaming thalwegs
    depths of the eocene sea

the   same   nakedness   of   life

            one single

r   e   s   p   i   r   a   t   i   o   n

(EA 11)

If Gaspar often invokes the desert's spacious emptiness (*"the naked tables of the winds"* [73], "familiarity with the void beneath the scattered names" [7], "sand limitless NOTHING" [4]), as above, its desolation is also a scattered plenitude of living creatures, plant and animal, here specifically named (barillas, anchorites, lizards, gazelles) in a specific geography (the plains of Sam, the Euphrates) and a breadth of erudition (psammites, thalwegs, the Eocene Sea) that is characteristic of *Earth Absolute*. So too is the epic lyricism coupled with the abstruse vocabulary of the verse: "the hand illuminated on the regs" (*reg*: an Arab word connoting a certain form of rocky desert), and the poem's spacious last line, which can be seen to *breathe* in the desert of the page:

r   e   s   p   i   r   a   t   i   o   n

"*I seek a respiration at the bottom of the stones,*" writes Gaspar (EA 90). The stones *are* the desert, the quintessential place of wandering, its burning sands

> worked working without respite
> in the atelier of the millennia —

at last, marvelously light and polished
crystalline bodies close to perfection
harder than steel… (EA 17)

The stones are also the individual poems in *Earth Absolute* — worked, working without respite by the poet, as a comparison between the first published version of the text (1972) and its revision, ten years later, will show. This translation contains the poet's revised version (1982), which offered its translator, in addition to the usual conundrums (e.g., what does he *mean?* how can I possibly say that in English?), the challenge of Gaspar's extraordinarily specific multiple vocabularies and the plethora of proper nouns included in his poems and his autobiographical essay in at least three languages: Arabic, Hebrew, and French.

The endnotes to *Earth Absolute* are the poet's. Where a note seems to be called for and doesn't exist, he has not supplied one.

Nancy Kline

LIST OF WORKS CONSULTED

Glenn Fetzer, "Lorand Gaspar: Poésie à la rencontre des sciences neurocognitives," *French Forum* Vol. 38, Nºs 1–2. (2013).

———. "Lorand Gaspar et la parole arborescente." Ibid.

Jérôme Hennebert, "Le livre de poésie et son morcellement: *Sol absolu* de Lorand Gaspar," *Le livre et ses espaces* (Presses universitaires de Paris Ouest: Open Edition Books, 2007) 337–357. http://books.openedition.org/pupo/510. Referred to in this introduction as J H.

Lorand Gaspar, "They tell me...," *Sol absolu et autres textes* (Paris: Gallimard, 1982).

———. *Sol Absolu* in *Sol absolu et autres textes*, ibid. Referred to in this introduction as EA (*Earth Absolute*).

Daniela Hurezanu and Stephen Kessler, "Between Poetic Vision and Scientific Knowledge: Lorand Gaspar," Translator's Note to Lorand Gaspar's "Poem" from *Nights* (Cerise Press, 2007).

Laurent Margantin, "Respiration de flûte dans le poids du calcaire. Entretien Lorand Gaspar / Laurent Margantin." http://remue.net/revue/TXT0310_MargGasp.html. Referred to in this introduction as LM.

———. "Rainer Maria Rilke, Lorand Gaspar et 'l'autre rapport'." www.oeuvresouvertes.net/spip.php?article104.

Marina Ondo, "Lorand Gaspar, faire la lumière sur l'origine du secret." www.larevuedesressources.org/lorand-gaspar-faire-la-lumiere-sur-l-origine-du-secret,1336.html. 20 décembre 2013.

Earth Absolute

"They tell me
I was born in 1925…"

They tell me I was born in 1925 in a small town in eastern Transylvania, whose acquaintance I was able to make a few years later. My parents met there, following the war of 1914–18, though both hailed from the harsh villages of the high Carpathian plateaus; my father had come to find a job after his discharge. As the child of novice city dwellers and happy to be so, I eagerly waited for vacations when I could return "behind the back of God," as they used to say. I had great affection for my maternal grandmother and for my uncle B., a bachelor, the only member of my family, it seemed to me as a child, who hadn't betrayed our origins at the heart of the peasant-warrior tribe once stationed there to defend the countryside against the new waves of invaders from the East, which Asia continued to pour into Europe. I later learned that on my mother's side I didn't have a drop of the "Székely" blood (the specific name of those Magyars of the mountains). My maternal grandfather was Armenian, and in my grandmother's family a German dialect was spoken. The only thing lacking from the mosaic was the Romanian element.

After earning a business degree in Germany, this uncle B. had returned "behind the back of God," where, as my father said, he demonstrated without even trying that he didn't have a head for business. I loved him deeply.

He was a sort of Taoist philosopher, speaking little, laughing easily, meditating habitually behind the eternal cigarette, happy to be alive, drinking heavily. He died a few years ago, at the age of eighty-six, "behind the back of God," stripped of everything except his good humor. To me, my grandmother seemed entirely transparent, small and thin, dressed in grey and black. I never heard her raise her voice, still less complain; she was all attention, all devotion. She died alone amid the final tide of World War II, which had taken far away from her all of her ten children and their numerous offspring.

These two beings reigned over a small universe of animals, barns, granaries and cellars, carts, ploughs and harrows, not to mention all the clutter of tools, nails, ropes and cans that filled the workshop. Behind the stables ran a mountain stream where the village boys taught me to catch trout under the stones with my bare hands. The great forests of fir trees were several hours away on foot, and among the mountain shepherds there were those who knew how to tame bears & leave them at liberty.

Some twenty kilometers away, a handful of graves were left to speak for the ancestors on my father's side. Widowed immediately after his birth, my grandmother had sold the little she possessed, in order to raise her two sons. By taking in the neighbors' laundry, she had managed to educate the elder son, killed in the first battle of World War I. She had placed my father in a little seminary, which he escaped from at the first opportunity, to hire out as an apprentice mechanic.

"THEY TELL ME I WAS BORN IN 1925..."

The only memory I have concerning this paternal grandmother is of an early morning, still very dark and cold — I must have been three or four — when my parents bundled me, half asleep, into a large black car unlike any I'd ever seen before, telling me: "We're going to Szárhegy to bury your grandmother." My memory has retained only the black of the car, the cold of a night not yet dispersed, and the mysterious idea, encountered for the first time, of death.

My native town, of forty thousand at that time, is built on the banks of a river where we used to swim in the summer and ice skate in the winter. One hour from our house, on foot, the slopes of the mountain were steep enough for skiing and sledding. Between the joys of snow and our wild races on the skating rink, which didn't close till ten at night, I wonder when we found time for our homework, during the four winter months.

My father had come a distance since his escape from seminary. He had the virtues needed to succeed in business, starting from nothing. A continent away, in America, he would have been a self-made man like those I later came across, who recounted their exploits in countless books. He had their energy, their perseverance, their intuition. I think his not emigrating to the United States after the war was the only regret of his life. Since Transylvania was not America — most people can't even place it; an American lady, who knew nothing more, informed me it was Dracula's territory — my father thought the knowledge of several languages essential. He saw to it personally that I learnt the three languages spoken in our country, & he added a fourth when I began primary school: French. Apart from languages, I needed to know math and physics, all the rest being merely literature. Doubtless he was unaware that the man he'd put in charge of inculcating in me the foundations of this new language (we called him The Parisian because he'd studied music in Paris) talked to me only of literature. As soon as I was capable of understanding it, he read to me or had me read aloud Letters from My Windmill. As for my high school French teacher, several years later — in one of those miracles that happen in little towns at the end of the world whose monotony is unbroken, aside from a sporting event or a moral scandal — he invited two or three of his pupils to his home and there initiated us, this was the supreme recompense, into the mysteries of Rimbaud's poetry. With equal enthusiasm, I followed the flights of oratory of our Hungarian literature professor, who found my sentimental attempts at stories not devoid of interest. As for my father, he considered with a mixture of indulgence & anxiety these first foolish efforts, published in some little magazine. As long as my grades in the hard sciences were good, it wasn't too serious! The day when, at thirteen, I confided in him that I wanted to become a physicist & a writer both, he looked at me long and hard, the way you look at a species you have vaguely heard about but never before encountered, and then with a smile to mitigate my suffering (or his) he uttered the oracular: "What I have taken so much trouble to construct, you will destroy!" The prophecy came true without my even trying.

"THEY TELL ME I WAS BORN IN 1925..."

In 1943, I'd been admitted to Budapest Polytechnic; my father couldn't have been happier. That didn't last for long. The victorious Soviet army was approaching the frontier. After a few months of intensive training, I found myself behind a gun, which was supposed to help slow down the invasion of Russian tanks. Of this war, I have nothing to tell, beyond my astonishment at having made it out, my departure occurred in a closed cattle car, which carried me toward some unknown destination in Germany. We'd been informed that, following an attempt to negotiate a separate peace in October of 1944, our government officials were seized by the SS of Skorzeny, who installed the Hungarian Nazi party in power.

It was my first trip across Germany. All I saw of it was a sky almost entirely filled with smoke, the interminable march of telegraph poles, the dirty walls of some railroad switching station, in which we were stranded for days, and wide open landscapes where we were strafed by Allied fighter planes. This somewhat peculiar form of tourism ended after a month in the barracks of Swabian Franconia. That I descended unhurt from the train was a new source of astonishment to me, soon followed by many others. When in the month of April 1945, the Allied troops had crossed the Black Forest and were closing in on Stuttgart, the confusion became so great that it was possible to organize and effect an escape. After two weeks of playing hide and seek, we were able to emerge from our burrows: French troops controlled the region. The commander of the unit holding Pfullendorf had us provisioned and ordered us to present ourselves in Strasbourg. It was a magnificent walk through Württemberg and the Black Forest. I remember the German towns half in ruins and, all around them, the jubilation of nature. A year later, after many other tribulations, I arrived in Paris. It was once again spring, the chestnut trees in the Luxembourg Gardens were flowering, people were smiling in the streets, I told myself the word freedom had a meaning; it was the most beautiful day of my life.

There, I found a small group of young people from Central Europe who wanted, as I did, to remain in France. Devoted members of the Hungarian diaspora in Paris and their French friends helped us to find work. Cook, valet de chambre, longshoreman, door-to-door salesman, night watchman, and so many other makeshift jobs seemed somehow miraculous to my comrades and me, in comparison to the labyrinth from which we were emerging. When I think back to those early Parisian years, which, seen objectively, were hard, all I remember is a joyous ferment, a long feast of friendship and mutual support. How many new faces, how many new ways of seeing and living! What open-armed generosity, after so much hatred and aggression! Though working, in October I was able to enroll in P.C.B. [premed studies in physics, chemistry, & biology], and then the years of medicine succeeded one another. Where did this altered course come from? The idea of medicine had arisen and then grown, little by little, developing deep within me along a hidden path. I saw in it, naively, a kind of synthesis

"THEY TELL ME I WAS BORN IN 1925..."

between two poles that never ceased exerting an equally strong attraction on my mind: art and science. It wasn't as simple as that.

You could feed yourself on very little money: a loaf of bread and some eggs, pasta and French fries. Once a week I went to reconstitute my reserves — caloric, proteinaceous & affective — in the home of a classmate's parents, who filled me with good things. It was harder to find cheap housing; many students of modest means had nowhere to live. One day, an enthusiastic and determined group learned that the old brothels, permanently closed under the Marthe Richard law, were not in use. The students stormed the one in Blondel Street, and the government ended up giving them three: Communal Houses were born. A friend who was active in the group succeeded in getting me admitted. That was the way I became, in 1947, one of the tenants in the formerly celebrated Sphinx, on the Boulevard Edgar-Quinet. We formed a republic that was colorful from every point of view, and hard to govern. Just collecting the rent, even at unbeatable prices, was a drama. As for chores, they regularly fell to the same people: those with the lowest tolerance for disorder and filth. Other conflicts arose from the varying demands imposed on one group or another by the course of studies they were pursuing. Between those who really had to wear out the seats of their pants and the joyous band of party animals revolving around a few art students, civil wars flared up, followed by ceasefires celebrated in common. This was a most salubrious experiment in social living.

When we came home every evening, the ladies whose house we had usurped were always there on the sidewalk, faithful to their posts. We knew them all. Our conversations were limited; our curiosity must have seemed incongruous to them.

At the outset, medical studies looked interminable to us. Very quickly we were forced to recognize they'd been too short. In 1954, a notice in the staff room attracted my attention: the post of surgeon in the French hospital in Bethlehem was vacant. Several months later, I set out with my wife and three children, of whom the oldest wasn't yet three years old, in a DC 6 headed for Beirut. In space and time, a new phase was opening. I was impatient to know those cities, those sites, whose names alone were enough to animate fabulous scenes in my mind. Damascus, Aleppo, Antioch, Tyre, Sidon, Jerusalem, Jericho, Jordan, the Red Sea, the Sinai, and how many others! I was going toward an encounter with a prodigious past; I received — full in the face and in all its continuity — the living reality of a multiple and complicated present. The purity of the millenary landscapes' song carried the violence of men's passions with immutable serenity.

On that first stopover, the Lebanese capital gave away none of its secrets to me, nor did the country reveal its charm. I was stunned by the convoluted mobility of the crowds in Beirut, delineated against a timeless, occasionally dreamlike backdrop. The strength of its contrasts, the dynamics of its contradictions offered me the initial elements, superficial *but meaningful, of an ambitious and fragile construction. In one hour's time you passed from snow-covered summits to the sea, in a few minutes from sumptuous neighborhoods to slums; there were as many mosques as churches. Later, returning there often, I loved to stroll through the old market neighborhoods, lulled by the sounds and smells, observing all the scenarios offered so lavishly by life in the souks of the Middle East. I would think of the Phœnicians in* The Odyssey *who "carried heaps of charms in their black ship." I would imagine the colorful turbulence of the ports, of the trading posts in the ancient Mediterranean world, besieged by those merchant-navigators, "famous sailors but rapacious men," the Tyrenians and Sidonians. In Damascus, as in Jerusalem, Aleppo, Baghdad or Cairo, merchant traditions were very much alive, but Beirut in some sense encapsulated them all. You would enter a shop "just to take a look at something," to purchase a trifle; a quarter of an hour later, over your most energetic protestations, you had all the treasures of Ali Baba's cave displayed before your eyes, while, conquered but content, you sipped an Arab coffee scented with roses. And if in the midst of all these marvels you had the strength to find nothing to your taste, you could, after a bit of conversation, leave without getting yourself insulted.*

It was a DC 3 that took us from Beirut to Jerusalem. We arrived from the east — that is, over the desert — after having gone around Israel. Full summer had moved into the Middle East, the airplane flew low over the bare hummocks, the rhythmic beige & brown of the great sensual undulations that were the mountains of Ammon and Moab, separated from the Judean range by the deep cleft of the Ghōr, where I caught glimpses of the slender, sinuous vein of greenery that accompanies the Jordan to its outlet in the Dead Sea. Offspring of a country of forests, what was there in my make-up that resonated so immediately with the vibration of this desolate land? In the course of the years, each time I came back to it, after a longer or shorter absence, the perception of these meager colors, these curvatures, these mesas, these rhythmic faults, unfolding as would a fugue, flooded me, physically, with the same simple and unutterable joy... I was in love with this country.

The DC 3 landed on a minuscule airstrip in Old Jerusalem. Driven by a very modern young sister, a prehistoric jeep took us along, stopping on the upward slopes for the engine to get its breath, toward Bethlehem. Cut off from Jerusalem's southern exit by the "partition," the Bethlehem of that time was a graceful town of some nineteen thousand inhabitants, surrounded by a swarm of little villages, hills planted with olive groves, vineyards and orchards. As we arrived, I was shown, on the right, the tomb of the exquisite Rachel, the favorite wife, who died somewhere along the road of return (from Mesopotamia or Transjordan), while giving birth to Benjamin, Jacob's last son. One example among a thousand others of those sites whose possession is contested by the regionalism of traditions. The book of Samuel (10:2) situates this same tomb near Bethel, on the territory of the right-hand son.

"THEY TELL ME I WAS BORN IN 1925..."

The hospital was located in the modern extension of the city, to the northeast. From our house, between pine trees violently contorted by the prevailing winds, I could see the houses of the village Beit-Jālā, embracing the summit of a hill planted with apricot trees.

Occupying three sides of a rectangle planted with gardens and bordered by a colonnade, the hospital buildings had been constructed in the 19th century. The church and the sisters' residence formed the fourth side. The charms of this conventual architecture were scarcely a match for the demands of a modern hospital. Still, with a little bit of organization, good work could be done there. Two times a week I reported to the French hospital in Jerusalem, taking a twisty little road that followed, from above, the Valley of Kidron; at its highest point, near the village of Sour-Bahr, in clear weather, I glimpsed at the very bottom of the vast frothy slope formed by the mountains of the Judean Desert, the mirror of the Dead Sea. When the city [of Jerusalem] was partitioned in 1948, the French hospital had ended up on the Israeli side, of no particular use on the margins of a hospital system that lacked for nothing. With enormous pluck, the sisters of Saint Joseph who directed the establishment had reestablished themselves on the Jordanian side, in a somewhat dilapidated old hotel to the south of the hill of Ophel, where archeologists place the site of the city of David.

The hotel-hospital was situated in the hamlet of Saint Peter in Gallicantu, overlooking the village of Shiloh. The church of the same name had been built above a cave dug deeply into the rock. One of numerous pious traditions claims this was the prison where Jesus spent the night after having been interrogated by the High Priest and the Sanhedrins. An improbable hypothesis, but there is a staircase there that descends toward the piscina of Shiloh and that must have existed at the time of Christ.

The location was difficult to get to, the premises hardly appropriate, and the sick numerous. Funds were obtained that permitted the construction of a new hospital. Scarcely a year later, thanks to the incomparable energy of the sisters, the project was realized. Light and spacious buildings, a modern set-up, welcomed patients henceforth on the heights of Sheik Jarrah, in a new neighborhood situated to the north of the old city. We moved from Bethlehem to Jerusalem, where most of the surgical work would be concentrated. The current reversed itself: apart from emergencies, I went two times a week to Bethlehem.

What to say in a few lines of those fifteen years lived in Jerusalem? Everything there enthralled me: my work at the hospital, archeological expeditions, the swarming life of the old city, of the people, the history of this earth.

From time to time, to escape the hospital's presence, grown too obsessive, I left for a desert. That of Judea began at the bottom of our garden. You needed only to go around Mount Scopus toward the north, to cross the line of crests in the Judean chain near the village of Isaouyia, and to let the Bedouin horse find his way, habituated as he was to pebbles and rocks, toward the Ghōr. In the winter, the oasis

"THEY TELL ME I WAS BORN IN 1925..."

of Jericho offered a haven of sweetness to anyone descending from the heights of Jerusalem, which was lacerated by cold winds. The descent of 1200 meters, which took twenty minutes by car, landed you in another world. There, only gardens and paths, the sound of water and golden dust. At Elisha's Spring, today called Ein el-Sultān, at the foot of the site of ancient Jericho, I would look at the procession of women coming to get water: a ritual dance renewing itself every day for nine thousand years. And all around, the desert kept watch. It was the desert, with its sandstone, its marl, its limestone, that gave and still gives the light its carnal touch, as in Jerusalem.

I loved to go there, too, at the height of summer, toward the end of the afternoon, when the unbearable furnace of day was giving up its last flames, to observe from the flat roof of a house of beaten clay the slow progression of the twilight on the great round folds of the slopes, spreading toward the base, of the "mountains over there." The last horizontal rays of sun, burying themselves behind the Mount of the Fortieth, disintegrated slowly on the surface of the Transjordanian plateau. Even farther beyond, I used to return to the great deserts of the east which extend with one single breath as far as the Euphrates. Or again, taking the southern routes that begin in Amman, I would descend toward the ancient Edomite kingdom erased by the Nabateans, that semi-nomadic people of Aramean origin, completely Arabized during the Roman era, enriched by the trading of myrrh and incense, which was bought by fortunate Arabia, if we are to believe Diodorus. Farther to the south lies the territory of Qédar or Cédar whose black tents — like the dark complexion of the beloved — are today erected by the Cherārāt tribe between the Sirhān ouadi and the el Hedjer, at present called Medaïn Calih. There, another Nabatean city may be found, less well-known than Petra: facades and rooms sculpted into the sandstone of a cirque of mountains emerging from the sands, pure lines left to silence and the work of time. We are already on the eastern shores of the Red Sea, in the middle of Hedjaz, at the northern limit of the Nedjd.

What has become of my old friend Abou Salem, who taught me so much about the secrets of the Red Sea, when, the felucca loaded with a good supply of water and rice, we left to explore by sea those banks bordered by the bare mountains of Genesis, whose granite, porphyry, limestone and lava compose infinite variations on a sober theme of beiges, browns, and russets? Diving in the world of "corals" is a constant fascination, quickened by the mute fear that the unpredictable moods of the sharks inspire. What a riot of colors and forms, what force of invention, what diversity of detail, what precision in the shaggy design of the reef habitat! Angel fish, lady fish, surgeon fish, stone fish, imperial butterflies, sergeant-majors, flying scorpion fish, parrot fish who graze on coral, clown fish stretched out in the fateful arms of sea anemones; and you, sea swallows, of so violent a blue, who keep a dyer's shop on the corner of a little street between hydroids and acropores, I can still see you bustling *around the client's jacket, floating back and forth, your fins stretched wide.*

What a contrast with the impoverishment, the surrounding destitution of the earth! And yet that nudity, that erosion of noble tissues, of rich parenchyma, gave me a still clearer perception of the tranquil pulsation of life. In this expanse, animals and men whom I got to know gradually revealed what was essential. Often, as night was falling, our campfire attracted visitors: scorpions, but also Bedouins. I wanted to know the life of the latter, camel breeders who still practiced seasonal migration over hundreds of kilometers. In approaching them, I was able to measure the price they paid for their freedom of movement, their refusal to submit to any law. The laws that were imposed on them by the harshness of conditions were, in my eyes, harder than those of the city. In the unwritten code of these spaces, the rules of hospitality, of assured shelter, had the same force as those of vengeance, as those prescribed by the rigors of the climate and the frugality of their economy. Pride, the honor of being full members of this pure kingdom of expanse were, for those I knew, feelings sufficient and necessary to their happiness. When it was a question of defending the reputation or the physical patrimony of the tribe, these noble hearts were, on occasion, shameless predators.

One day, amid the excavations of Qoumrān, I met one of them who had chosen the sedentary life. Small, quick, intelligent, he was a poet, storyteller, and excellent cook.

At the end of the dig he came to see me in Jerusalem & said to me point-blank: "Hire me, you won't regret it." He was right. We separated from him thirteen years later, when we left Jerusalem; we felt as if we were abandoning a family member. He died a few years later, of cancer.

I would need the space of a book to try to bring to life so many faces, to try to render some small part of the joys, the agonies, the passions experienced with such intensity, the inexhaustible hunger I felt in myself to explore, to discover, to know. Eventful, that's what these years were, often to the point of exploding, filled with liveliness and suffering, revealing — what, exactly — what relationships, what elementary movement of the depths, what more essential language?

Two months after our move to Jerusalem, the announcement that Jordan was about to join the Baghdad Pact caused a wave of insurrection. We were living temporarily in an apartment on the first floor of a building whose ground floor was occupied by the offices of UNRWA and whose second floor housed the Consulate of Turkey, one of the treaty's member states. One morning, while we were breakfasting peacefully and in all good conscience, a mob stormed the building. Stones began to rain down on all sides. We had just enough time to barricade the heavy front door and take refuge in the bathroom, the only room in the apartment which had no window, the ventilation duct being unlikely to let in stones. It quickly became obvious that stoning wouldn't be enough to appease the attackers' passions. Soon,

"THEY TELL ME I WAS BORN IN 1925..."

they broke down the front door and invaded the apartment. Already having witnessed scenes of violence that cost lives, I didn't think ours had much chance. I desperately braced myself against the bathroom door, blocking the handle, which by chance was mounted backwards. Fortunately for us, the primary objective was to raid the apartment. What couldn't be carried away was meticulously destroyed. At the end of half an hour, which felt like an eternity to us, along with cries of victory accompanied by the disquieting smell of smoke, we heard several bursts of machine gun fire. We were liberated by the Bedouin army; the flames from the library, ignited with gasoline, were beginning to reach the rest of the apartment.

It was a little later that, attracted by more clement shores, we set out to explore the Ægean in fishing caïques. The volcanic islands here were often as bare as our deserts, and the lives of the fishermen scarcely less harsh than those of the nomads. Still, how weightless everything appeared to me, how airy those villages, raised so frankly in the light! Thus it was, in traveling from island to island, sustained by our fish, that one day we took refuge in the harbor of Patmos.

Between the rock of Patmos and the stones of Jerusalem there was a common denominator: the light. It was undoubtedly sharper between the white walls, the magmatic rocks of the Ægean islands, more golden, closer to the blood, more mutely imperious and corrosive in Judea, but both returned to that same clarity of ferment that you saw, in both twilights, arising in things.

Oh, the mornings in Jerusalem! There was such coolness, such promise in the break of day, in the stones, that I quickly learned to get up early. I would make myself a coffee, water the horse and give him his first meal when Khalil was late, then I would turn to my books, to my scribbling. This meant I had, each day, two or three miraculous, transparent hours, before embarking on a long day at the hospital. The little I've succeeded in reading and writing I owe to those Jerusalem mornings, to those Judean dawns which began to emerge at four o'clock, in the summer.

Nevertheless, the situation in the Middle East kept getting worse, the tensions growing. Ever since my childhood I had known the unbridgeable chasm between two discourses opposed to one another by a passion for one single good, between two narratives exclusive of each other, mixing up facts and undeniable arguments with invention and the utopias of the imagination. During the Six Day War, in 1967, the French hospital found itself in the middle of a battlefield. The surgical team did not leave the operating room for several days. I see us still in that tragi-comic scenario, in the middle of the night, working under weak emergency lights, attuned to the shriek of missiles, clinging to the table whenever a too-close explosion sent us its breath through the demolished blinds, while, as we looked on in amazement, at every detonation our sweet instrument sister disappeared beneath the field of operation; we restrained ourselves with difficulty from joining her. One week later, when I was able to make my way as far as my residence, not much farther

"THEY TELL ME I WAS BORN IN 1925..."

than a hundred meters from the hospital, I found the door staved in and the house looted.

Two years later, tired of a life complicated on a daily basis, I accepted the proposal of a surgical post in the hospitals of Tunis. I left that country, Jerusalem, with death in my heart. That light which had become a little my light. I had grown up among these stones. I did not regret one minute of those sixteen years: it was simply time to migrate. I have only congratulated myself on this decision.

I finish writing these pages, which leave me in the greatest doubt as to their interest for anyone but me, before a window open on a gloomy sky. No trace, today, of those colors of a melancholy beauty that the two expanses unified by my horizon know how to wear, in winter. Just tattered grayness, unknown in tourist posters. Yet, between this house on the steep slope that threatens ruin and the great ocher-russet stones of the riverbank, an almond tree completes its blossoming. But I have to leave, they're waiting for me at the hospital.

Sidi Bou Saïd, February 28, 1982

I wrote these lines for the publication in Poésie/Gallimard of three of my texts: *The Fourth State of Matter, Earth Absolute, Corrosive Bodies*. At the beginning of the book will be found, in the guise of a reflection on poetry, several excerpts from *Approach of the Word*.

The Fourth State of Matter has been so thoroughly revised that it is in fact a new entity. In my mind, this new version does not replace the first; rather, it constitutes a different development, at the level of language, of the same experience fifteen years later.

As for *Earth Absolute*, apart from some additions or deletions thought necessary for the coherence of the whole, the changes in no way alter the meaning of the original text.

Approach of the Word

The language of poetry cannot be enclosed in any category, cannot be summed up in any function or formula. Neither instrument, nor ornament, it scrutinizes a word transporting the ages and the fleeting space, founding both stone & history, the welcoming place of their dust. It moves about in the energy that makes and breaks empires. It is this dilapidated backyard, overgrown with grass, its walls covered with lichens, where the evening light lingers a moment.

No one justifies poetry and it needs no defense: I am only trying to see what in myself, guided by precision, goes in such an unchangeable way toward that nightly groping, toward the search of another, a rockier precision. To understand and not, to knock up against, to break, to lose oneself and still to understand. I want to assume all the contradictions, to exceed them. For everything in me knows that I am speaking always the same language (that which *speaks me, constructs me* in speaking, in expressing) on different levels. And it isn't a matter of more or less perfect degrees of elevation, higher or lower: what distinguishes them is a particular movement, a particular nameless organization, a relation to the human and the world. The abruptness of a proof without name and the patient methods of a fragment.

I see no break between the language (or expression), which is the differently enlivened matter, human discourse, and society. Levels of emergence, of composition, of vitality *&* desiccation, perhaps of sickness, of a same word that shows itself in discontinuous signs, caught up in the game of a formidable combinatory, a game whose matter, rules and energy, text, syntax and writing, it is.

What my ceaselessly interrupted word is seeking, ceaselessly insufficient, inadequate, breathless, is not the pertinence of a demonstration, a law, but the laying bare of a gleam that is ungraspable, transfixing, of a fluidity in turn benevolent and devouring. *A breathing.*

To class, isolate, fix; these exercises guided to their somnolent usefulness, now we are ready for the sleeplessness of genesis.

All these paths I am following open onto something impossible where only the vertical exercise of the word maintains the motion: menace, happiness, *&* loss. And nowhere any term that would resolve, reassure. Nothing but this narrow pain; nothing but this excessive width. You cannot close off poetry: its central place collapses upon itself, in a compacity that consumes itself, makes holes in itself. An unfounded silence where, against any proof, the fragile word, the scandalous word, the crushing word, the useless word still moves forward.

The poem is not an answer to a questioning of the human or the world. It only digs into and aggravates the questioning. The most exigent moment of poetry is perhaps the one where the movement of the question is such — by its radicality, its bareness, its irrefragable progress — that no answer is expected; rather, all reveal their silence. The breach opened by this gesture effaces the formulations. The separate values, duly catalogued, that create the coming and going between opposite shores are, for a moment of lucidity, caught up in the force of the river. From this word that refers to everything that is burning, the mouth lost forever.

Our meaning and our thought are ceaselessly encumbered with reflections, losing this vivacious fluidity that we sometimes call soul. But someone stops near a dilapidated wall of mud, near a stone where words are lacking. He palpates the seed of an off-white, secreted light. He touches a porous crackled glass, with the rough texture of the voice. Moving through the strata, he works in the very motion and breath of language. An architect of the statute-book, he shapes the material of signs at their birth. Ceaselessly taking up again the veins of an order at the source of their energy, he leads them to a meaning that disappears. This endlessly thirsty seeker, this eternally inadequate person, this scorner of the impossible is above all a worker of language, a worker despairing and laughing. Going to the very fibers of the weave, to the sources of the chemistry, he wants first of all to gently wipe off the vapor, *the vapor of the vapors*, to look through this ungainly hole at the slow migration of the landscape.

Poetry is sometimes capable of conducting (like good metal conductors) a quivering of language, communicating to words its fluidity, its corrosive and forgetful power. So the word — the image — transforms itself from a simple chemical element participating in the constitution of a composed body (a *seme*), into an enzyme able to operate the synthesis or the *lyse*, the unexpected creation of new compounds, which raise, in what burns them, different flames.

This place of high energy, where words are ordered, which we call poetry, is our part of the infinite act in the world, a force field of the laws of our own motion, where our constellations are composed *&* undone.

Here is a molecule that provokes the saturation necessary for the formation of a crystal, an enzyme that unleashes such a construction, or "recognizes" elements that without it had no meaning, at least not the same one.

And here is this breach opened by a sound, a relation of words, a joining of images that permits us to see where formerly we simply looked. To breathe where we only talked.

The person who is capable of setting alight those gleams that can be born from such articulations or such defeats in the constellations of language, who knows how to forge them, provoke them, that person, how could we not recognize him? In listening to him, perhaps once, we will comprehend without any frontiers.

To express oneself, to integrate oneself, to melt, keeping firm the thread of this singular movement. The full sweep of the weave envelops the disturbed dreams of the rocks, the fright of the depths. Capillaries of freshness of birth forgotten; lightness of the earth under the unexpected advance of a healing. Vast steppes and their reaches of tall grasses that rock the slithering of beasts, blood and space of a single melody; lovers, you who know how to go almost without leaving any tracks.

Don't look for the absolute. It is in you like a ravine of dryness that will lose you. All language plowing the earth bears its thirst. Love and doubt. Bitter grass and fruit, the pulse set right & defeated.

The poetic text is the text of life, worked by the rhythm of the elements, constructed, eroded by everything that is; fragmentary, full of gaps, showing more ancient signs in its faults. Texture of ardor and of circulation: everyone can read there *something else* & also the *same thing*. What we pompously call creative activity is only just a faculty of combining, of constitution of new ensembles starting with existing elements. What reveals itself really at some moments is a quality, a taste, a coherence and a disintegration proper to this new compound. But perhaps, to staunch this thirst for composing new bodies, to assemble no matter what to no matter what? There is something of everything in nature. Some persons find their happiness (or their "truth") in the strangeness of dream, of chimeras of the imagination, others are forever fascinated by life that moves, breathes, and does business (but it's also what produces dreams & chimeras), unfolds itself here, comes apart there. Still others try to name, to show through these so crumbly words, what has from always invented motion.

The central paradox, the absent key of a certain poetry today is that it tries to break into a domain where the logic of language stops short. Modern physics has had to admit a similar failure of ordinary conceptual language when it was a matter of saying, for example, how an atom went about emitting or absorbing light.

It might happen that the clear water of a language between the words of a poem would send us back to the origins of all tongues and of all language, an augural domain which calls upon us like an unexplained disquiet. There is a vein of energy that is language, that makes its continuous way from cosmic dispersions and geological folds to the weaves of life, to the most abrupt motions of the imagination and song. When voice reveals itself there, an inseparable motion, it's as if it recognized a face, a modulation, a fundamental relation proposed by the world; as if our language were to throw together all our architectures of stones and winds, suddenly plunged from the present to the ages without memory, recognized its unknown act. Recognized itself.

At the threshold of this indecisive day: the poet with his small pouch. Naked in this desert. And naked to the point of a scream and desperate to lose all meaning. Who will hear him in the atelier of unusable dust? Even here, in the laudable work, who will perceive his silent excavation? What place to anticipate, avid as we are of brightness outside, for a lamp that simply breathes? This man has nothing to propose that will transmute excrement into gold, which will transfigure the misery of outside into the currency of salvation. Nothing. Some words in a rude foreign language that he understands as a native tongue.

But what poet has ever doubted that language was a river in the river and breath in the breath?

To pursue the poetic process into its last refuges, to hurl it above the last wall of words which break the stride of the herald. Where the discourse, too timidly, there leans over an abyss of language.

To write a poem that would not be an abstract of traces, a translation or formation, a waning of the different levels of the lived, of its prodigiously entangled arborizations — the writing of a reading at another level —, but a growth and a motion both simple, issuing from no center and no beginning, its branches, its leaves, its fruits not being there to refer to anything else, to symbolize, but to conduct the sap and the vivacity of the air, to be their humming and their activity, nourishment and seeding. And reading would no longer be the deciphering of a code, receiving a message; it would no longer be a matter of reading from your observer's station so prudently exterior, but rather of flowing into the unforeseeable progress which is, with a similar gesture, the motion and its laws, the difference and the identity, the form which is constructed and undone. Reading *&* writing: to welcome, to accompany, to dig, to breathe, to flash forth.

The Fourth State of Matter

KNOWLEDGE OF THE LIGHT

Our rivers have caught fire!
A bird sometimes glides over the light —
here it is late.
We shall go through the other end of things
to explore the clear face of night —

I know mornings mad with their stretches
of desert and of sea —
motion reshaping faces
refilling its traces.
Monastery of life of pulmonary flame
in the smoking thickness of noon —
we teach the algæ, the fish
the color of air and the story of man
to set them laughing in the evening in the opaque ink
of the frightened squid

THE FOURTH STATE OF MATTER

this morning coming so freshly in your eyes
still full of fragile porcelain
the porous day
its long wool kiss
this whole body remaining somewhere for the night.

Light plays in the narrow bodies of birds
brief motions of air where sounds pleat and
reveal the skin   the eyes of women

men heavy with trespass, with sleep,
night arched in their backs are looking
at this mesh on the water severed by the slightest things
and over there surely some windowpanes afire —

THE FOURTH STATE OF MATTER

white walls of rested birds
fossils by chance in the layers of day
waters painted with our passing
the depths are still trembling —

swaying of wings
rapid chasms under the skin
one leans over smoking beaches
with cheeks burned

tender cloths of grey steel
our hands pruned on the slopes
of this light —
and our fingers laugh
at wheels immensely slight
in the most inward house of life
where someone comes
steel
silence
folds.

THE FOURTH STATE OF MATTER

Sounds swell in the tiles of light.
You've made yourself white night in the white
piercing the net of our sounds.
Distant surfaces devotions
days fritter away in the arena
and the gaze
and the dance —

I have built you from screeches & cries
exhumed then slowly
buried once again.

Blinding slowness
from mineral to the sea
long trips gouged out in time
to find yourself in a plant, a ciliate
the coolness of its nights
all those doors where you are and give up.

THE FOURTH STATE OF MATTER

Like those astonished gazes
at being dead
as the drunken birds
tear off their feathers
our gestures were too clear
to not surprise
their weight in shadow.

LORAND GASPAR

So far off that the smile does not know the eyelids.
Drawn from the long cries of birds in flight
the fluid letter of unremembering things
the day burned you might forget the words.

THE FOURTH STATE OF MATTER

Over there at the end of the world
over there the suns
the swollen mouth of nights
over there horizons
the wild silk of desire

grave world
where nothing's insulted or ugly
the knife falls
the day walks on the ceilings
in its copper entrails.

The port is repainted black
there are two or three very white boats
where night is lacking —
windows where islands
sunken in the eyes are dreaming.

Oh so much night eaten away to white
we also had a fate of window
where someone cried out with joy —
silence the port at evening
two or three very white boats
where night is lacking —

THE FOURTH STATE OF MATTER

I wanted to be loved —
exact beggar at the feasts of light
worn out with grey & blasphemies.
From this flesh I keep the bones
of so many stitches —

now the daytime
        the naked eyes
                and someone
has repainted my ceiling of things
and already I see nothing more there —

THE FOURTH STATE OF MATTER

it is raining in the sun
the trees & houses are graver
by the earth weightier I know where you are
when the eyes are emptied
and you see space through them.

ICONOSTASIS

Light from far off.

I would like to breathe freshness into you
   capillary by capillary
that bring forth the slipping of air
   and the tightening
of the papillæ   make green words for you
   in the morning of words
that you feel like touching crushing
to write you with nails in the lazy age
    of rocks
in the eyes —
to convince you about the earth.

The sea
the evening
the bodies
interior walls of touch
to pluck from the roughcast stomach of birds
the unrolled surf and the same brief point
the taste of green almonds
and bitter tobacco.

THE FOURTH STATE OF MATTER

Lips wounded with burns longer than the day —
this tingle *&* this delicate noise
of mesh clacking in the vertical air.
Grasses scarce
and the patient eye of voracious fish
in the somber mud of the depths.

Clearing of forces in the treeless evening
severity of the continual.
Only the steps, these fugitive camps
of an image right in the stone.
The fall of the angel in the fires
the flame at the edge of the bodies
that of my fingers in the rigor of the faults
great leaf of the day
fossil of night.

THE FOURTH STATE OF MATTER

These metals I curve in my voice
so you'll exist in the dark.
I have emptied the night of its brilliant rubbish
and I hear the stampede opening again
a whole lung inside the stones —

It happened that someone put a face
at the borders of our steps
to put it to sleep.
Sleep under the still warm skin
sleep under the vault of the roofless birds
along the bodies
to join to split apart
we experienced the motions of the sea
and were broken with thirst.

THE FOURTH STATE OF MATTER

Having of a sudden lost our ancestors
their skulls we carry and where we sleep
the smoking bones around the faces
in the aged smell of incense & bread
under the burning limestone of the monkish cells
our hands undid the dark and the words
returned to the single clarity of the body.

Light of fingers at the approach of faces
do you know the Khmer forest?
I didn't see the trees
the clampdown at the heart of the stone
of one more depth.
Migration of furniture of walls & of steppes
then the unbearable precision
of halts of squares of houses.

THE FOURTH STATE OF MATTER

Oratory in the stone slowly gone cold.
In the white of our eyes the dark room
with all its chemistry biting the faces
the day was so long
with its chalky winds and bones
the night broken so many times
by the brief gestures losing color —

The extreme patience filing us down.
The bread of a day and the measured water
the excess of keeping silent
and among so much white
finding by groping
the narrow paths of our veins.

THE FOURTH STATE OF MATTER

Here are hands
place them in a brief tremor of your body
with a pot of basil
and space pecked by birds
when the dawn on our moistened bodies
our fingers smell of oregano.

LORAND GASPAR

I have only very simple things
the sun is sliced bit by bit as
my mother sliced bread
we are putting soup on the table
(these things outside which are slowly falling,
jasmine, snow, childhood)
the taste of red peppers and of joyous teeth
our bodies still keep us warm a while
in the advanced age of night.

THE FOURTH STATE OF MATTER

What strange landscapes compose your voice
embroidered in the rooms I no longer know
what rooms I walk teapots through them
and branches of unclothed trees
the tea is smoking or perhaps the garden
perhaps also the bottom of the icons
the lightness of things perceived by the ear
the skin pleats in some places
the porcelain of the cup is getting cold
we are waiting
the windows take the color of eggplant
then close the night

distance has come into the nighttime room
where a gesture or two have loved the light —
the bodies stand up in the invisible brightness
of bare hips and syllables of water
long & brief of the mouths leaning over
noise of glass wrecked on the depths —

but how to say the love
the disaster and the beginning
the time curbed under the infinite watch
and the debris of plaster
encrusted under the skin —

the evening again this clarity of stones
a life that rises from nowhere for ever
forest of hands and gropings in the enclosure
we enter the night clothed in our bones —

SHELLS

Death where so much life is lost
abandoned by our feeble eyes.
Torrent you astonish us
shining & muddy
from mouth to mouth
the sweet and the bitter
pebbles and wood
finished taken back.
These blurry photos
that time has moved.
The light seeks itself under our hands
and suddenly all is feather
snow snow —

The same wind pulled into the fire
the same night with the same texture of branches
of an unavowed joy.
The same growth in the gestures
and the bareness of hands under the skin
sudden gaps in the forms
when space hears us —

THE FOURTH STATE OF MATTER

We have just barely lived
the time of this weight
of all that rips itself asunder unlamenting
your view last night
and all these small ports of the eyes
the eyelids repainted.

For years we haven't traded
except with stones.
Our steps light up with blind chalk
thin layer between two points of water.
My life burned with so many lights
sometimes because of immense tenderness I forget
that everything is deaf
and I raise myself up like a melody.

THE FOURTH STATE OF MATTER

I listen to you
sound that burrows into the mornings
the very thin bodies
dance on the knives
standing sharp in the weft
of a resurrection —

LORAND GASPAR

Our lives ripened in the hottest of our limbs
all our dwellings on the move from now on
the obtuse thickness of our walls
from strand to strand and from sea to sea
porous and frail in the hand
and everywhere these shells
where the day trembles & decays

THE FOURTH STATE OF MATTER

I say now all is smooth *&* dismayed
I say by the bald mountains of memory
in the pleats of a great foam curtain
when the sea windows open
that the sky should fit facing the shadow
and the skulls of the passerby be readable —

How far shall I stretch to watch over you?
You teach me to walk when the path is silent —
Don't forget this white wood of windows at evening.

Night circulates along its vast nets
its pupils dilate at a constant speed
and never burst —
you'll never reach
the depth of this night

THE FOURTH STATE OF MATTER

trembling obstinate fevered detail
I read your rigor in the shadow of depths
everything is so smooth so clear so rested
no disorder or anger
in the pure snow of laws
beasts at claws and at teeth
struggle in silence
between skin & light —

all this grandeur of air
is swallowed in gestures
everything that is not yet
comes so near in the straw
of so many extinguished worlds —

I know your steps wearing out in my veins
I know your step like the words I make
like what pierces my silence
and undoes itself.
You pour nights into my limbs
and leave me
when day runs into my lamps
to remake yourself from nothing

THE GARDEN OF STONES

We were living in the coolness of going
bearers of images to the garden of stones
the vast empire spread out, exposed.
What remains in the breadth of years
breaths gone blue, limestone violence
enormous land of mute lives
green crackles in the fingers of chalk
little by little we learned to listen
somewhere to the fall of jasmine —

all these nights in the stones
you sleep your eyes your lungs steeped
with sounds of a wind forever.
The limpid flood of a fugue of bodies
leaning on the hours that harass the bed
of the hasty campground in the light —

to silence the names with enough joy
so that the lines of force
show up in the gaps.
See if you can feel the artery
of so much weight —

THE FOURTH STATE OF MATTER

There were nights of crumpled steel
set with gestures curved in the fire
the weight of sands & sorrows forgotten.
Patient skylight in the thick of shadow
at each dawn in the granite of the heart
you learn again to move the light —

This sound of words
that you came to dry up
on these paths where the wind
readies with cares the minutiæ
of an entomologist stooping over butterflies —

what I used to love most of all
the grassy clarity of fragile joy
it was then the invention of the stem
thrust forth bravely, vulnerable
only busy at growing.

THE FOURTH STATE OF MATTER

That in so sweet a syllable
I can dilute all violence and all gold
this pure wheat of myself gone quiet.
The crumbling is at my fingers —

I feel you like an inflection in my voice
where the dusts of evening come to rest.
The crossing will be long said the angel
in the thickness of the stone

THE FOURTH STATE OF MATTER

let there remain just the sole eye of our weight.
We were forever coming back heavier to earth
pierced by space nailed with light
our hands quieted in the fall —

your arms fall
in a low-lying purplish forest
your eyes fall
and the scales of your voice
and I listen to myself a thousand centuries on
recomposed sound by sound.

THE FOURTH STATE OF MATTER

I hold my life
a piece of bread
so hard the hundred grams
of the prisoner of war
and often I'm so hungry
that there's scarcely any left
and things are colored
in marvelous fears —

Night again.
Squall of windows in the bodies
sudden & mute.
The painted flame of the voluble day
its powders placed on the icon of flesh
and each step of the evening to grasp
the exhausted memory how long will we delay?

This fullness almost and the ruins of lighthouses
the waters inside knock against the panes
immobile I hear my hearing myself somewhere
an inexhaustible hunger to be born —

Earth Absolute

To the naked song of the Judean mountains which revealed itself to my thirst on the pathways of Rock-strewn Arabia, desolate & blessed.

SILENCE

STONE   STONE

still another

STONE

sand

limitless

NOTHING

Altars
stelæ
dolmens
cromlechs
kists

       (thick blocks of stone whose massive cubes
      cover their ancient sepultures)

or a simple P i l e of S t o n e s in witness of

       an understanding
       an accident
       a crime
       a death

    TORTURE of STONING

       closing up a well
           the mouth of a cistern
           wall of stone
           tower of vine

c o r a l t o m b s o f P e t r a .

Magi
Caravaners
Bandits
Traffickers
Onagers of men

       ON THE BURNING ROADS

                myrrh
                incense
                gold
                pearls and stones

    ON THE ROAD WITHIN SIGHT OF NOTHING

the enlightened   the clairvoyant   the blind

"My brothers have deceived me like a stream
like the bed of the seasonal wadis
whose waters swell with snowmelt
and run dry in the burning sun.
For them the caravans leave their routes
plunge into the desert and are lost — "

ARABIAN PENINSULA
HEDJAZ

g r a n i t e
        porphyry
                limestone
                        volcanic outcrops
                                rivers of lava

ḤĀRRA

s u l f u r   j u m b l e
                iron ore
                      copper
                          silver
                            word

ḤAMD

T e b ū k
    T e i m a
        el H e d j e r
                e l – E l a
                      M e d i n a
                            M e c c a

HEGIRA

from the Great Harran of Ḩaibar   to Jebel el Kora

                        familiarity with the void
                        beneath the scattered names

EROSION

>	works whose passion is the same as
>	the coherence of matter
>	language of innumerable rhythms
>	displayed crumbled recomposed

CHEMISTRY

>	of w i n d s
>	of w a t e r s
>	of d r e a m s
>	of l i g h t s

the same movements compose and elucidate
the breadth of the trajectory without intention

more than once at dawn,
>   in the desert of Ram or of Toubeig
>   or   farther   south   along   the   shores
>   east of the Red Sea in that place where
>   pink granite veined with lava, tender sandstone
>   and blinding gypsum slow their slopes

I have dreamed of a genesis
>   the universe was emerging without interruption
>   not of an order that came from outside
>   but ample but full of its music
>   at being there   infinitely compact pebble
>   filled with the dance that vibrates in each sound
>   drilled into the light —

a fugue of clear and shadowed curvatures
>   without beginning or end

poured out from the outpouring
>   at the same undivided pace
>   breath doubled
>   on the pulmonary paths

the force of silence
>   of which these deserts at dawn
>   are the unfolded leaf
>   the rustling cool — disclosed —

>   or again
>   on the chalky rotunda
>   of the day's last arenas

the speed of the light
>   abruptly penetrated by the languor of a caress
>   the murmuring of hands beneath deep skin

like water from the eyes
>   that renders faces a blur —

EARTH ABSOLUTE

Good morning to you who come in the night.
Good morning to you regal approach that splits the pulp of the sun.
Good morning to you in the dust.
>All this day to wear yourself thin, to wear the day thin.
>To the bones of your weariness.
>When the light bends over a well —
>Peace, noises settle down.
>Ah, how hearing smooths out!

Goodnight to you who come in the light, who come as silence.
Like a final eyelid of color or of sound
You migrate in depth, leaving the pallid day on the embalmer's table.

desert

    what remains of music
    when the design is no longer visible
    as if light had eroded
    the time and the place that belong to things
    as if the grammar of the depths were readable
    by the hand illuminated on the regs

a n c h o r i t e s

    lizards

        s n a k e s

            hyenas *&* cynhyenes

    through the morning's gorges
    on the evening's slopes

the unmapped roads of solidarity in motion

    the wild oryx
    the Arabian gazelle

the wind across the plains of Sam south of the Euphrates

    barillas
    shrivelled shrubs
    sandstone plateaus
    sheer-cut psammites
    streaming thalwegs
    depths of the eocene sea

the   same   nakedness   of   life

                one single

r   e   s   p   i   r   a   t   i   o   n

Stretched between the crest of the Judean range and the depression of the Ghōr, the desert of Judea displays its undulating slopes to the east, like an ocean swell solidified on the immense carboniferous sea.

This orientation shelters it from the humid winds out of the west and exposes it to the scorching breath of the eastern winds.

Rare gusts of winter sweep into the riverbeds deeply sculpted in the cloak of hard rock. The runoff filters into the porosities of the senonian limestone, whose strata are badly joined. These subterranean waters irrigate the oases nestling beneath the steep walls of the Ghōr.

Yet at the end of even a parsimonious winter you can see hilltops of a blinding nakedness covered with a timid, sparsely scattered green that perfumes the gaze. "Let the desert and the arid earth rejoice, … let her exult and cry out in joy."

Soon the first Ḥamsīn winds make sure to burn the tender down along the flanks of the hills. Then summer leads the landscapes back to their absolute source. Exemplary fate between the brilliant whiteness of the chalks and the reverberation of the overheated browns of the rivers of flint. The pulverized rock pushed by the east wind raises its mud cataract into the arrogance of the blue.

Approaching the crest you encounter the biblical midbār, a region of semi-desert, a zone of transition where nomads graze their skinny herds, and the fellaheen push their wooden plows between the loose stones that shelter wild cyclamen. Once arrived at the end of his "field," the farmer gazes for an instant, through his mule's legs, at the blue trough of the Dead Sea, scarcely bigger than that sparrow hawk suspended over the fractured fault.

LORAND GASPAR

THE FLINT OF DAYBREAK
KINDLES THE MOUNTAINS
AT THEIR ROOTS

WE WILL SEARCH THROUGH THE CLEAR STONES
TO THE UTMOST LIMIT
OF THE DARK.

EARTH ABSOLUTE

I come from the revealed core of this unavowed walking:
Judea of my shadows, how you dance at the height of day!
The broken sun your stones disclosed to me,
their depths of trees never born
greens without leaves in the thickness of the winds
without road and without rose —
and the empty spring beneath the funerary stone,
so alive that it makes the marble porous,
that the pigments of light emigrate
in the heavy breasts of night.

FLINT

> like a somber and warm origin dispersed
> poem-deserts in the light of evening
> stripping duration naked before the eye

>> flint finely veined with quartz nodular flint whose silica has contracted into an ellipsoid block englobing a fossilized organism, the debris of clay and chalk. Sometimes, the silification of the core being incomplete, the cavity that's left fills up with percolated water, to produce crystals of calcite or of quartz.

"Then Zipporah took a flint, cut off the foreskin of her son and touched it to Moses' sex, saying: Truly! to me you are a blood husband!"

THE FLINT OF THE EMBALMER

>> perfume of our roads at night
>> ah, the putrid garden of our entrails!

*Every morning at a bound
the sun sure-footed on my face.
I take hold of that burning as if a rudder.*

Grains of sand

        worked working without respite
        in the atelier of the millenia

at last, marvelously light & polished
crystalline bodies close to perfection
harder than steel   in the war
of all against all   indefinitely
they revive without ever wearing out

        These great deserts of sand
        offer us loose soil almost en-
        tirely crystalline from which
        are absent the silts and clays
        so indispensable to organic
        growth. And yet, microbio-
        logical research demonstrates
        the permanence of microflora
        in the harshest sands.

Compact impenetrable sky.
The earth is caught in the hardened tables of its law
which sends the gaze
back infinitely behind its source
to the liquid skeleton of its song.

LORAND GASPAR

EOLIAN SANDS OF NUBIAN SANDSTONE

    high russet waves
    of the dunes at Dahna
    snowy mælstroms
    of the sea of Safi
    red sands of Nefoud

the horizon flows at the speed of a river

    sharp slicing carving images
    the days roll polished bursts
    translucent globules of silica
    on the line of the water of the crystalline
    roll their peaceful fire
    weeding the gaze the memory

EARTH ABSOLUTE

*Our urgent need to see in ardor stilled
has spent its quarries' credits, its horizons' foam.
To save one shore from the absolute landscape
for the heart to break on
we've had to disrobe again and again.
From the void rise birds of prey
pure of eye in the confused melee,
quicker than the leaps of your blood.
Where are you off to swearing between restive donkeys
that you proclaimed light?*

Pliny the naturalist tells how some saltpeter merchants having stopped to rest in a sandy region: "finding no stones on which to raise their cooking pots, used for the purpose loaves of saltpeter from their wares. When this saltpeter under the effect of fire mixed with sand spread on the ground, they saw the flowing of transparent streams of an unknown liquid…"

EARTH ABSOLUTE

*You flow with the day
raising straw from the hard ground.
Trace of fragrance of fire
and of air this body dispersed against
the sheer weight of the universe.*

*Once this breath, this word
this gesture at the edge of its own movement
sprouted from a sweetness like this
of solitude broken.*

NUBIAN SAND STONE FROM THE ROYAL CAVES

"Rudiste marble"
"Nérinées marble"

Stones of the Temple

> "the king ordered the extraction of huge stones, valuable stones, in order to place on great stones the foundations of the House —"

Quarried stones

> with which Jonathan later fortified Mount Zion —

those admirable stones, twenty cubits long, ten wide and five high

> that Herod's architects used, Josephus tells us, to erect his palace, his towers —

And the soft limestone called Kakuli

> resounding beneath the hammer's shock, sometimes it is covered with *blight*. "When you have arrived in the land of Canaan, which I give you as your domain, if I strike with blight a house you own there, its owner will go warn the priest and say: I have seen blight in the house."

EARTH ABSOLUTE

If despite rough-casting the blight persists, the house will be demolished, its stones, its structure, and its rough-cast walls will be transported to an unclean place. As an offering of atonement the priest will procure

>two birds,
>some cedar wood,
>the red of cochineal &
>hyssop

he will sacrifice one of the birds over a clay pot above the spring tide. Then he will take up

>the cedar wood,
>the hyssop
>the red of cochineal &
>the living bird

and plunge them in the blood of

>the sacrificed bird
>and in the spring tide —

And after having made the expiatory sacrifice of the house with

>the blood of the bird
>the spring tide
>the living bird
>the cedar wood
>the hyssop and
>the red of cochineal

seven times will he sprinkle the house then set free

>the living bird

outside the city —

𒁉𒁉𒁉𒁉

מִדְבָּר

𒁉𒁉𒁉𒁉𒁉

ش

الصحرا

*We lived among the brambles bordering our terrain
in the shattered panes of the summer storm
wounded blue by the shards of sea
all the way to the groundless ground of nights pronounced
suddenly beneath the fingers that follow erosion
and behind the flesh that hastens in the voice*
the blood translucent, so much did it open
at the end of its broken slender stalks —

Thus you discovered fire.
At the very bottom of your humid pulp prolonging your paths
without hope of a trace farther than your fatigue.
You made of it this hole in the splendor of the visible.
The charred tree of leafless space unfolded its stars.

The landscapes of your vision emigrated so high in the winter
your hands are more tender now
with this warm ignorance of the earth closed up again.
Ah, how well they know the muffled voice
that swells and evaporates in the clouds of dust
when it falls on the perfumed ear of the witness.

STERILE EARTH
   inhospitable earth

one day, after so many years of not waiting
like a divine promulgation   a cloud
too heavy to pass breaks: it's the flood

  In the humid mud

    as a billion years ago

  in this first garden

    protozoans leave their shells
    insects their cocoons & chrysalises
    seeds swell up until
    sleep breaks

  in a cracking of clay

    the timid soul of a green shoot

  salutes the light

    how the hills are encircled with joy
    and the flowers

  what temerity

    what self-confidence in life
    what scorn for all that isn't
    the intimate flesh of movement

  tender shell of finished light

    kissing the harshness of the earth

he who hasn't met you

    will he know to hear
    the clarity that sometimes vibrates
    between words —

'Black flesh to fool fire'
Iris of the desert
Iris of that same melody
that dissolves the touch
between two indecipherable pages of the day.
The gaze steeped in arising
groin of another pleasure
slowly you drink your death —

*We were seeking words to run through vast expanses
where the light leans over and trembles for an instant
on the cancelled threshold.*

*Sparse paths of our eroded secrets
there the heat takes to its bed
beige lawn of our tentative gropings.*

*Perfumes from which gardens did you come to dream on our limbs
where we were licking the dust from our wounds?*

*From well to well
from mouth to mouth
we kept our faith
in a deep garden
stratum of sap
buried scents
blossoming beneath the earth's back
yet from one well to another
absence grew sharper.
The feverish water of the halt
gave it the flash
of exterminating angel.*

EARTH ABSOLUTE

*The day swollen with weariness seeks out our faults
the split clay at the back of our mouths
the first green shoot of our humidity
and how our laughter stirs it!
The blueprint of a wing pressed into marble
the voice cut off, silenced, forgotten.
Yet somewhere there still flows
the song's joy that unfolded at a bound
the space forever morning's —
the nine celestial vaults bend
to the fountains of our sap run dry.*

Insects

born of the same rain that
brought a whole flora out
of nothingness, the light
as though slowed by this
buzzing, transport the
pollen from anthers to
eyespots, couple and lay —

plants

the only beings that connect
directly with solar energy, as-
siduously fabricate organic
food with just a little water and
some carbon dioxide; without
them, no animal life —

birds & lizards

eat insects and seeds, time
their period of reproduc-
tion to coincide with this
double effervescence —

of a billion seeds produced
within an area 4000 m², only
a thousand or two will make
it to the next rainy season.
Most are gathered up by har-
vest ants & rodents, relatively
few by birds.

If rodents and lizards have
had enough to satisfy their
appetite, snakes, hyenas,
and coyotes will not want.

> The   seeds

>> know for sure when it is time
>> to germinate. The right amount
>> of ground water, a good tem-
>> perature of soil, and there they
>> are, they swell, speed up. Still,
>> even when all the favorable
>> conditions come together, not
>> all seeds answer the call. Each
>> species stores up a reserve this
>> way, taking the measure of the
>> fickleness of the sky

> thorns

shriveled, harsh leaves,
above all no useless out-
pourings, not a hint of
those displays of certitude,
of a happiness invested
in broad surfaces. Work
in the sharp, the narrow
cultivate ellipsis. And yet

> the succulents

>> sumptuous in their edema
>> drunk on juices hoarded be-
>> neath barbed waxy raiments —

and those dowsers who
thrust their taproots down
as deep as thirty meters in
the alluvial terrain —

> onions tubers rhizomes

>> two thimblefuls of eau-
>> de-vie, bitter and tenacious —

Splendor of a Stapelius
variety of fatty plant
of the genus Caralluma
whose flowers give out
a nauseating scent
In this way it attracts
from miles around
those good highflown creatures
those fat flies more sumptuously
clothed than Solomon in all his glory
Calliphora Lucilia Sarcophaga
who usually find their happiness
in putrefying organic
      matter.

The sacred scarab
>	servant of the Sun God

conscientiously rolls
with its back legs
its precious pellet of

>	manure

Sometimes the female meditates balanced on her ball. Often two join forces for transport and for the feast that takes place in a shelter dug into the ground. Astonishing digestive tube! This fine canal, of a prodigious length coiled up consumes every last organic molecule of the skimpy residues abandoned by herbivores' intestines. With the first mouthfuls, the slim blackish filament that appears at the level of the anal orifice and unrolls without interruption until the end of the meal, which lasts from 10 to 15 hours, is smooth as silk.

>	When the time to lay has come, the female chooses the richest the creamiest excrement that she can find, with which to fashion not a ball, but a pear of exemplary proportions and finish.

> It is in the narrow part, in the neck
> of this ripe fruit that she digs the
> tabernacle (the comparison is Fab-
> re's) where the egg will be deposited.

THE ARACHNIDS
> scorpions
> spiders
> galeodes
>> are creatures of astonishing efficien-
>> cy, designed to hunt and to consume
>> the insects they absorb almost daily
>> in quantities equivalent to their own
>> weight.

THE BURROWING OWL

can subsist for a whole season
without drinking. He nourishes himself
with juicy spiders.

> Twenty or so species of

fish
> live in the desert, in hidden
> water holes fed by thin
> ever-flowing streams; others
> appear in the ephemeral

torrents
> of the rainy season.

Their eggs hold out against
several dry seasons, buried
in the cool depths
of the earth. The

burrowing toad
> born of the last rain, the minute he feels the humidity decrease, digs a deep hole, backwards, where he shuts himself away for eight to ten months, in other words, until the next rainfall, if it proves faithful to their rendezvous. Then, hastily he digs himself out, settles down beside a precarious puddle and dutifully begins to utter heart-rending cries to wake up a female somewhere. Not a moment to lose.

The revived female immediately lays her eggs which are fertilized without delay. The young hatch at the end of a day or two, hasten to reach the bottom of the pond in order to complete their metamorphosis. And already it is time to bury themselves.

> Athlete of hydric asceticism, the

gerbil
> lives in subterranean hideouts where it heaps up stores of seeds. It never goes out before nightfall. The saturation of the subterranean atmosphere helps it to minimize its loss of moisture through exhalation and to recover some of this lost humidity. It is free of sweat glands, hardly urinates, and produces excrement that represents perfection in terms of hydric economy.

A gerbil can live out a
whole gerbil lifetime
never having tasted

    water

> Many animals of the desert, especially rodents and birds, practice a form of summer hibernation, which consists of falling into a deep sleep that permits them, thanks to a lowering of the organism's temperature and a diminution of all biological rhythms, to reduce their caloric and proteinaceous needs to very little.

Pliny thought that the camel disposed of a mysterious reservoir that permitted him to do without water for long months at a time. In fact, it's hydrogen produced by the decomposition of reserves of fat accumulated in the hump, that, combined with the oxygen of breath, gives him this capacity.

EARTH ABSOLUTE

A LIGHTNING GRAFT
               YELLOW GOLD ON GOLDEN OCHER
ON THE NAKED BELLY OF THE SANDS
             THE VIPER INJECTS
GOD'S VENOM INTO THE NIGHT

*Impatient to break the horizon for another
the same farther along   the farther land
where nothing more is helpful.
And our endless fall the same curve as the air
in this empty median of waiting for a tree
the bird has come to rest somewhere in space:
see how he dismisses the prow of the heights!*

*Where words are present
this gully in the dance'
each day defeats
the spokes of the wheel.*

EARTH ABSOLUTE

EARTH & SKIN
SCORCHED

the mouth & the eyes
    dispossessed
    stripped

space of a cry
               surrounded by
space
               surrounded by
nothing

أيام وليالي نهيم
على هيكل تأكل من جسد الأرض
في أنوار المدى والحجر الصغراء
وفي غباء الجسد والورود
يندّ عن عطرنا عبير ياسمين وحبّ
دون امن سليم نفح العبير

*The perfection of the spheres
one day we'd seen it
tremble in our hands.*

*Timid counterbalance
when eloquence runs dry
ah, the reptilian lamp of our bodies!*

And certainly
> the immensity is in me

the joy of going into the clear of the rhythm
that attunes and separates the sounding cells
with the speed of space toppling over

> its breadth of light

spurred on with no halt or well except itself
circulating freely outside and within
you having only this time and this place
here in the stones to illuminate
> intermingled
> extradited
> disrupted

the dust so surly on the tongue the eyes
so fluid the good fortune of words
the confidence of the body in the music
the tongue ceaselessly broken, pegged

> with a frightening and fortunate
> amplitude

the journey restored to the journey
the whole length of this supple road
the soothsayer examines the manure of evening
predicts the night at the heart of man
predicts the flame of the immemorial waters

> unfettered expansion

"That is why I will allure her
bring her to the desert
and speak to her heart."

*How your muteness grows in the face of my eloquence!
How you veil yourself with transparence when I pursue
a certain word in your veins!*

OUR HUNGER VASTER THAN THE DESERT

"Blame your mother, blame her!
For she is no longer my wife and
I no longer her husband.
Let her banish her whorish desire
from her face
and adultery from her breasts;
if not, I will strip her naked
as the day that she was born
I will make her into a desert
a desolate land
I will kill her with thirst."

LIMITLESS THIRST IN THE LIMITED THING

Color of flesh risen in the somber bread
Mountains of the other shore, Edom, Moab.
Door of my eyes in stride toward the abrupt
loss of the straight path
like the circle broken by the prey beneath the eagle
which you don't see in the distance.
There, walker and stone commingle their erosion
space flung negligently over one shoulder.

> For the men of the Sumero-Akkadian &
> semitic civilizations in the west the desert
> appears to be a place not only cursed but
> also the domain of destructive subterra-
> nean forces. At least that's how it's shown
> us in the ritual attached to certain myths
> concerning the death and resurrection
> of Tammouz (Sumero-Akkadian) or of
> Al'iiân Ba'lu (Ugaritic). Some historians
> think that during certain periods of the
> Ancient Testament, Yahweh must belong
> to the same type of divinity.

In the "liturgies" of Tammouz, EDEN
is at first described as a verdant place.
It is the eruption of enemies into the
sanctuary (this "place of the people,"
this "place of life"), delivering it up to
pillage and destruction, finally to the
god's abduction, which causes EDEN
to become a sterile, deserted place.

> And yet the place where the aggressors
> lead Tammouz is likewise called EDEN.

> "He goes, he advances toward the bowels
> of the earth, in the land of death the sun
> is rising for him"

Moved by the divine abduction
Ishtar bends over the devastated land:
> "Brother, the crushed verdure,
> who submerged it, who crushed it?
> . . . .
> in their resting places,
> you've destroyed the sanctuaries
> of their depots, their stores,
> you have made pathways and I the Lady
> you see me wandering
> among the bedouin Sheiks"

Evening opens its scroll of Psalms
the voice melting to blue on its bedrock of lava
recites the bottomless mountain of finitude
the bald heads of the mute assembly.

Take off your sandals you on the threshold
of the kiss that will set you ablaze!
And what is this shipwrecked coolness
in the light of your eye
where each day Canaan is engulfed?

Violent, these nights so close to morning.

You come by the great parched rivers of Ethām
in the stupor of midday which sends us back
beneath our tents, but how would you come
into the porous shadow to share our hunger
when all the expanse is the same flame.

I hear the step on the debris of light.

MAR.TU   AMURRU   SA.GAZ

       Ḫabiru   ʿApīru

In Palestine the fortified cities of the civilization of the Bronze Age are destroyed one after the other toward the end of the third millenium before our era by bellicose nomads who will camp for two or three more centuries in their ruins.

> Toward the same epoch, the Egypt of the First Intermediate Period and Mesopotamia after the fall of the third dynasty of Ur, now vulnerable, complain of nomad incursions.

The names MAR.TU (Sumerian) and AMURRU (Akkadian) which refer to them on cuneiform tablets mean: *people from the west*. Doubtless it's a matter of the same nomads, spread throughout the Middle East, starting from the steppes of Syria, known today under the name of Amorites. (Not to be confused with the Amaru / Amorrheans, a name given in biblical texts to a segment of the pre-Israelite population of Palestine.)

SHÛ-SÎN

> the penultimate king of the III dynasty of Ur, "built a rampart against MAR.TU," a wall of the West
> that "pushes back MAR.TU's force into the steppes." In the epic of Lugalbanda and Enmerkar it is hoped "that the MAR.TU who do not know wheat will be diverted from Sumeria and Akkadia."

ACHTOÈS III

pharaoh of the 10th dynasty, alerted by his son Merikare against the incursions of the evil Asiatic "who does not live in one place; his legs are always in movement; he has been at war since the time of Horus; he does not conquer and is not conquered."
Let us note that the names of certain of these Asiatics established in Egypt belong to the semitic group from the northeast, the Amoritic names. We will find these same names in
texts of execration.

SINUHÉ

going into exile across the desert, mentions in his narrative the
wall of the sovereign
built probably by his master, the pharaoh Ammenemes I "in order to stop bands of foreigners from descending on Egypt, begging as they do for water to give their livestock."

(One thinks of the Great Wall of China, built likewise in the 3rd millenium, against the Huns.)

The tablets of Mari mention names of many other turbulent nomads: Suteans, Haneans, Benjaminites (not to be confused with the biblical tribe), and finally the Ḫabiru or ʽApīru. All these tribes are more or less related and the continuity between them and diverse Aramean groups of whom we hear for the first time in the cuneiform texts recounting the campaigns of Téglath-Phalazar I is probable; in fact the regions occupied by the Arameans coincide, especially in Upper Mesopotamia, with those of Amurru.

EARTH ABSOLUTE

ABDI ḤÉPA
AKHNATON

As for the Ḫabiru or ʿApīru, they pose a fascinating problem. They were spoken of in the "letters" (tablets) of Abdi Ḫépa, prince of Jerusalem, addressed to Akhnaton, whose faithful vassal he calls himself. In comparing Hittite treatises with the tablets of Rās Shamra in the same epoch it was understood that the ideogram (or pseudo-ideogram) SA.GAZ was the equivalent of the cuneiform Ḫabiru.

It is commonly thought that Ḫabiru or ʿApīru designated individuals of a social class rather than an ethnicity. Wandering without land, having broken the ties with their people of origin, their tribe, reassembled in more or less coherent groups of nomads, who raised livestock, they were also intrepid warriors. Their way of life required a mix of pastoral and military virtues; in love with independence, they were capable of adapting themselves to no matter what situation.

> The myth of the god Amurru's marriage speaks of a man "who does not know how to bend his knee (to cultivate the earth), who eats raw meat, does not own a house during his lifetime and is not buried after his death."

The root ʿpr in west-semitic means dust, corresponding to the Akkadian *eperu*. The ʿApīru were the "dusty ones" on the great caravan routes.

arammi obed abi

> "an Aramean separated from the tribe (was) my father"
> thus begins the prayer prescribed for the delivery of the first fruits (Deut., 26:5), one of the oldest in the Pentateuch.

On all the paths where you led
your flocks of doubts and hopes
your hand in the hazelnut softness of young camels' fur,
in the burning cisterns that recall
the belly of the earth — you know
beyond your stride resumed at dawn
in paddock dreams there was nothing to find.
Nothing except this vast no-place

nothing except the long sure step of your distraction.

Dazzling defeat of a migratory flight
the blue grass cut beneath the wings.
O the light caught in our almond trees!
Wonder
        to have been for one day earth's aroma.

Upstream from springtime
we came from nowhere, from never
to water the desert.

All is smooth
sky and earth cleared of their excrescences
all is vacant
at the advent of your absolution.
Lucid the chambers where you announced the blood.
Simple your writing you lie down in limestone.
Unveiling nothing: ungraspable fluidity
ravine of my eye which unwinds your light
your words decayed at the bottom of the urns
the same taste of salt that erodes my sight
and the eye cries out beneath the stone of the gaze.
What was there to unveil?

No agitation in the work
no sweat in the effort
immense thirst put to bed in its wadi.
Nothing remains except this deep red glow
in-you-in-me
rudderless.

Taa-Souît
> said the Egyptians
Earth of the Void
> these deserts between Egypt & the Promised Land
Badiet et Tīh Beni Isra'il
> desert of distraction of the Sons of Israel
> of the Arab authors
Midbār Šour
> Desert of Ethām
>> Dunes of el-Ğifār

2000 years before Jesus Christ Sinuhe the Egyptian, political exile crosses these deserts to reach Canaan:

> "Then thirst swooped down and rushed toward me; I moaned, my throat contracted, I was already thinking: this is the taste of death."

The Egyptian expeditions of the 15th and 16th centuries before our era set out from the fortress of Ṭarou (Tell el-Aḥmar), several kilometers to the east of el-Kanṭara, the starting point of the oldest strategical & caravan route toward Gaza. The army of Thoutmes III took ten days to cross the el-Ğifār along this route.

> A second route leaves from Daphna (Qom Dafana), on the other side of the lagoons; passing through Magdolum (Tell el-Ḥeir) it rejoins the Pelusian coast (Tell el-Farama). Alexander took seven days on this route from Gaza to Pelusium, the Roman legions five, going the opposite direction.

Plutarch will say the soldiers of Gabinius feared the road from Palestine to Pelusium more than war.

> In his campaign against Egypt, Essarhaddon requisitions all the camels he can find in order to confront the Ğifār; the bloodthirsty sacriligious king Cambyses succeeds in his victorious descent toward the Nile Delta where he defeats Psammitichus III and becomes Pharaoh, thanks to the bedouins who wait for him at every stopping-place with their camels bearing skins of water.

EARTH ABSOLUTE

*Somewhere in the groin of the dazzled provinces
the green of the tactile reign.
Eyes, hands recaptured softly in the dark bulb
in the fatal heaviness of the fruits of the earth.
When at last the day
and its faces that separate us from the stones
have disappeared.*

*Leaving the sky at its windows,
between our lips and our arms
the nameless awakening filters through.*

To indicate the desert
>   the Hebrew of the Bible most often uses the term

> midbār

the stem d a b a r : to lead to pasture refers back to a primitive usage of this word. It indicated lands that, when the rainy season ended, might offer grazing to the flocks.

The Assyrian m u d b a r u or m a d b a r u
has this same meaning of zone of transition

> The pastures of the desert drink
> and the hills are encircled with joy.

> Deprived of the humus needed to retain the water of a brief exultant spring, this rash vegetation is quickly erased.

the cantata of curves
of croups and flanks
of Judea, of Moab and Gilead
dressed in golden shimmers
of the skin, until within the
grip of triumphant summer
the earth displays the brown
and beige fibers of its desiccated flesh.
>   Negeb from the old semitic root *ngh*
>   to be dry
>   *Arābāh* and *yešimōn*, from ערב and ישם
>   to be arid to lay waste

> places at once terrible and sacred
> where you meet
> savage beasts and your own
> heart

For ancient Egypt
> the desert is a *world of exile*, an "exterior" world
> (for the French of the Middle Ages, *eissil, essil,*
> often means "destruction, ruin"),
> over there in the mysterious West where to the aged sun
> the doors of a kingdom open, offering divine
> springs and ingredients to make it young again.
> Thus it will revive at the frontiers of the desert.

The hieroglyph
> that serves as a determinative in different notions of the desert is composed of three hillocks, separated by two valleys. For the inhabitant of the Nile plain, to go beyond fertile lands meant "to go up," to walk beyond the mountains bordering the plain.

This sign is painted in yellow ocher
or pink, spotted with russet:

> thus appears the shimmering pelt in
> brilliant light of the slow undulations
> of the deserts of sandstone and of limestone
> between two blinks of the eye.

Unclothed modesty of this chalk hip
when the dazzle quiets down.
Your path held within its inner glint
the name perpetually recast.
The yellow unveiling folds back its nudities
toward darker swellings.
Under the searching xyster
here and there the skeleton of fire shows through,
not the blazing white wave of the Tih
but the calm frequency of dilated pores
which frost over as if seized by their own murmur
and this eye crumbling at the summit of the blue
(arid splendor in the hollow of the expressed)
where petrified birds sink like stones

What sweetness on the slopes of this slow return to earth!
Only our talk entangles the visible
arming itself under the fall of night.
Stars bustling.
But soon
beneath the intersecting vaults of gravity and silence
like a judgment dispersed in the equal light
the high and the low, fire and stone
smoothed with the same gesture under the soluble web.

For sanctuary
the slow saturation of your evening.
Sky of a single gesture which no longer stops the earth,
the backs of the hills made clear —
eocene clarity, its vast meadows of marl
ripened beneath the sea.
From all the dances and battles of shells
the soft gold of our eyes.
Just that. Just this
dark and russet bed of the incomparable. Nothing.
We will lie down for the only grass between our hands.

EARTH ABSOLUTE

Fold after fold
from fault to fault
deposited
searched
sparse'
dedicated to the same homeless depths —
patiently the day is dying.
One day I will have seen
this last dam of cyanotic light
dissolve in the smooth gray
of the pebbles.
And your wing was beating still in places
sudden whiteness which calls out
in the calm death of the embrace.

For the

HAGIOGRAPHERS

> pious city dwellers with vivid imaginations, the desert, which they usually don't know except by hearsay, is an arid land indeed, but above all filled with shadows and all kinds of terrifying creatures, satyrs and onagers, apocalyptic beasts —

It is a battleground between

GOD *&* SATAN

> a place naturally designed for those who wish to purify their soul, which only the temptations and attachments of the body hinder in its climb toward the light —

These men, in whom dwelled a limitless passion for the absolute, seem to have understood obscurely that it wasn't in this life they must unite their souls with God —

> Now, it proved to be true that the seductions of the

> city, its powers of corruption, so many times denounced by the prophets of Israel, were nothing compared to the temptations it was necessary to combat in a body crushed by deprivation. And the stronger the temptations, the more it was necessary to break, to diminish, to annihilate the flesh —

THEY BURNED WITH DESIRE IN THE
DESERT

"One day, at the approach of evening, the Seducer of men put on the form of a very beautiful woman who, in the guise of a wanderer in this desert and wearied of intolerable work, drew near the cave of John of Egypt and pretending to be exhausted, entered in and threw herself at his feet, begging him to take pity on her (…). John of Egypt, touched by compassion, ushered her into his cave and asked her for what reason she was obliged to wander thus in the desert. She gave him false but well-invented reasons and in the course of her story spread all the poison of her attractions, all the venom of her flattery, telling him sometimes that she was miserable, sometimes that she was not unworthy of his help. Thus did she touch the mind of the solitary one with the so pleasant sweetness of her words. Even sweeter conversations having followed on the first, laughter *&* caresses

mingled with them (...). She triumphed over this soldier
of Christ and made him her slave. For he began to feel
greatly troubled in himself and to be agitated by the impetuous movements of unregulated passion without the
memory of his past works being able to restrain him."

> These are very ordinary difficulties,
> which must be confronted almost daily,
> as long as one is not entirely dead to
> the world, transparent —

The monk Zosime, singing
the Psalms in the desert,
perceived a sort of shadow
of a human body

> it was a woman whose body was desiccated, blackened by the sun; she had
> hair white as wool which fell around
> her neck.
> "I beg you to forgive me, Abbot Zosime. I cannot turn toward you to speak
> to you, for I'm a woman and as you see,
> I'm naked…"

TO BE LIKE THE DEAD AND THE
STONES

Arduous are the paths
inhabited by monsters
and the softness that dwells in us
in the brotherhood of matter —

this road exists in the flesh
& the invincible light perceived by An-
thony, Pacome, and Macaire the great
luminary and great pneumatologist —

"One day Macaire was in his cell,
he looked to the right and he saw
there a cherub with six wings and
numerous eyes was hugely near
him. And when Apa Macaire had
thus commenced to look at him,
saying: "What is this? What is
this?" then in the splendor and
the light of its glory, he fell on his
face, the saint Apa Macaire, and
became as if dead."

"The monk in a state of hesychia is he
who aspires to contain the incorporeal
in the dwelling of the flesh. The cat
spies on the mouse, the mind of the
hesychast is watching for the invisible
mouse. Do not scorn my comparison.
You would show you're not acquainted
yet with solitude."

Draw from the fire that fuels the fire
strip the flame of desire
for it lifts the hills' foundation
for it devours the still heart

*You will be the salt of the moving waters
when the path and the eye have eroded
you will taste the last word of dryness
you will laugh at the final ruse of thirst.
Blossoming by your fevered light alone
— ah, how fragrant! —
your mouth filled with nights —*

"There is not the slightest pathway leading there nor any mark that can be made upon the earth to get there. But you proceed by observing the stars. Rarely do you find water there and when you do encounter some, its odor is very bad & smells like asphalt, but the taste is not disagreeable.

Recluses live there of an immense perfection, so fearsome a place being inhabitable only by men who embrace a perfect life and whose courage and confidence are proof against all things."

For this torrent without a bed
this immobile song of stones

For this narrow pain
this nerveless path

For this austere fire which ignites no tree

For this flame never born
that carries the darkness of my voice

For your unspoken name enchanting to my ears

For what remains to me of coolness
For this meal of dust

For this water rising
in the clearness of the stones

EARTH ABSOLUTE

To live nowhere in no time
to freely follow the veins' branching
the sparse shards of radiance

     keyboards of so many hoof steps
     and all a world shattered to light
     grassy rustling pebbles

in the journey without end unmoving

     there remains the PLACE deserted
     every place remains deserted

"in the palaces grow brambles
the viper will nest there, will lay
there vultures will assemble"

       letters & numbers in the same handwriting

Our bodies arched beneath the lash of day
night finds its streaming pathways.
Hearths that burn more densely
our melted gestures on this shore where
the sea swells in search of its concealed heart —
we already feel beneath the death of light
how morning's tender dunghill breathes.

EARTH ABSOLUTE

As a round presence in man's palm enlarges
his soul until it's gone from earth.
Along this fugitive slope
I perceive the naked tables of the winds,
the emptiness of your dwelling.
Origin and ending under the same sign.

You can do nothing to this night.
Blind white blinding in this dark.
The soft ash of your vision in the wind!
Sometimes you touch the clarity of what is crumbling
silence nothing more can hear.

My country is so wide that paths without respite
erase themselves cross take turns with each other —
lives traverse me and at times enflame me,
o the songs!

There remains forever
the always cool door
of the history of fire.

EARTH ABSOLUTE

*The warm joy that remains at having mixed
    our ferments in the stalk,
Our days exhausted in this bole of night
like a dawn of space on the shores of flesh
the bony bed where mornings tumble
under a gaze of grasses growing in the flames.*

As long as an

    ATHLETE OF JESUS-CHRIST

lives in this world —
    each of his victories raises innumerable
    enemy troops —

Whether they be nomads or anchorites
the life of men in the desert is a
d a i l y   b a t t l e

    THE APOCALYPSE
                        always begun

and I remember the dawns of Mōğib, of Ḥesā
landscapes of a world's beginning and end

    pulsation of the pores of granite *&* sandstone
    blinking of notes on the immutable staves

EARTH ABSOLUTE

This dawn again.

The abrupt glimmering on our hips.
Soluble lights, clandestine.
Tinglings in the numbed shadows,
doors, passages, unions.
In the dark bread of things
the mist of molecules resounding.
Vortices of woolly air, torn from them
minute planets of snow.

Unsuspected by a morning like this we keep
our words among the gently leaning flowers
curious beings of the thirsty earth as it deciphers —
The gardener unpacks his tools without so much as a glance
measures his hands, his water, his hope
in the growing clarity of stripping away —
while the day grows irritated in its radiance.
Without windows and without exteriors, the nail shines
in the exorbitant mechanism.
The depths have melted once again.
We travel from shore to shore incurable.

Bow down in the gray of dawn
toward the eastern shore of your coolness.
Sing in the face of the rising sun
your robe of day in which the humid flesh
of love and night arises to soothe
opens to welcome the fatal kiss
patched up with hopes and fears
Don your white cowl of the consumed page!

"The Arab and all the princes of Kedar themselves were your clients:

"They paid in sheep, male goats, and rams. The merchants of Sheba and Raamah traded with you: they provided you with aromatic herbs of the finest quality, with precious gems and gold in payment for your merchandise. Harān, Canneh, and Eden, the merchants of Sheba, Asshur & Chilmad traded with you. They traded in rich garments, cloaks of purple and embroidery, variegated cloths, thick braided ropes in your markets."

At the end of so many years lived in earth's nakedness,
   you were looking at the strange place of a tree.
You had seen the world made of great pages clear and
   inexorable
open to the stride of a breath without ties.
In this garden of olives everything was intertwined.
What did these twists and turns mean, these rifts, these
   joints, these shadows in the shadow beneath spar-
   kling eyelids?
You showed them the nakedness of your nerves, the
   weak lamp of your pain.
Fame and catastrophe at their loudest, can you still hear
the song of the sweet limbs of Jibrin, the porous rustle
   of your origin?

EARTH ABSOLUTE

Badia   Biddaoui   Bedouin

INHABITANT OF SPACE

    man without ties
    wanderer of eternal movement

To renounce everything that can bind, hinder walking,
make heavier the camels' load —
        to live on little
        without moderation
                in eye-splitting light
                      embracing the horizon between eyelids
camp broken before dawn
        to take up one's terminable path
        in the interminable radiance
                          walking
skins and textures where
the rustle of divinity is born
        a glass of cool water
        a cup of coffee
        an almond eye
               Your eye has marked my heart with
               stigmata and here they are identical
               wide clefts
        a spear thrust
on this nakedness of chalk and flesh
the undissectable breath of a pulse

to be present to abandonment to absence
blood relative of flint and sandstone
of untraced paths
of dawns' splitting
      the ardor of silence in the nocturnal home
      the quivering of water
of the storyteller's voice
the eyes shine with desire

LANDSCAPES OF GENESIS AND FALL OF ANGELS

Theology of the breath and of thirst
of the light that rises in bodies
in stones

EARTH ABSOLUTE

Morning of cools and of musks —
you offer your fruits to the stride of a beginning
your thighs still humid with desire, unclothed of gravity —
how faraway the song already of the burden of the camp!
How it washes the pores of the gaze!
Inhabitant of the gesture without dwelling
we wed the porches of the god
raised in the dust —

> *from one absent threshold to the other*
> *bearers of breath our bellies, our lungs*
> *smell of iodine, of yeast*
> *this weak movement in the joints of the night!*
> *No, no dreams!*

Our bodies know the frankness of the journey
innocence so keen whose only beat
nails us to the heart of a void —

Our clothes are scalding   the hardened
gaze sent back to its excavations —
sunk   melted   where the light branches.
The only way of seeing: a white lacerating pain
can you spread out again the heavens' vault
on this earth dancing damasked with steam
between the two optic nerves?
And yet the dew.
               It incubates in the muscles of fire
               it has its dwellings in the blackened crusts
               it has its speed in the pulsing arteries
                         in the white intensity
                         in the river of lava
                         unaware of the sea.

"I was devoured by the heat of day
by the cold of night
and sleep fled from my eyes."
             Sky of bronze
             earth of immobile fire
                       struck by consumption
                             by high fever
                             by rust and by blight
           for clouds, only stormclouds of loess
           the color of bile and damnation
           that travel the way ghosts do
           great tatters of dusty souls.
The dew in movement.
           In the boles of light
           in the dark canals of calcium
the day hidden in its skeleton of aromatic herbs.
           I have devoured the heat of day
           the nocturnal cold crackles in my pores
           like God's asthma
           sleep riddled with fires of frost
           the odor of stone kisses the dew.

EARTH ABSOLUTE

*Little by little our stones in the pulsatile reign
exposed a feeble trembling of entrails
of sleek nerves and timid skeletons.
And all the new gestures under the dew!
Watered by glimmers in the humid dark
ah, the fragrant blindness of the jasmine quarries!*

"If you see me, like an animal that lives amidst the sands exposed to the heat of the sun, in a state of poverty, barefoot and bereft of shoes, know I am a man devoted to forbearance; I hide beneath my armor a lion's heart, and for me the firmness of my soul replaces sandals. At times I lack for everything, at times I'm in abundance; for he is truly rich who does not fear exile and does not stint his life. Indigence and need do not tear from me any sign of impatience, and riches do not make me insolent. My wisdom is not the plaything of foolish passions; never am I seen to seek out the unfavorable gossip sown by fame, to tarnish with cunning reports the reputations of others."

> "When I take the earth for my bed, I stretch out on its surface a back supported by protruding dried out vertebrae, and rest my head on an emaciated arm, whose joints all seem so many dice thrown by a player, which stand up in front of him."

What shame son of the great emir that you've become a servant of these rouged and perfumed people, the food of the city has given you a paunch, a hump.

> How can you robe yourself in humility, be completely stripped of pride, after having lived free and glorious.

EARTH ABSOLUTE

*At the end of millenia spent walking in insomnia
in the exacting purity of morning on the earth
this my mouth will remember filled with limestone
and every morning woke us to its fragrance of bread
cooked on the random stone of the encampments
thus did we cross Šour, Ethām, Ğifār
carrying our lungs at arms' length all aflame
this evening without fault at last, ah, do not fall asleep
you could awake the light that separates —*

Naked sky of my birth, modesty of the song that bursts outside, with which the ignorance of my tongue joins for an instant —

soil baked by sun and frost   searched by brief waters of the winds' ploughshare which glaze your vision

like a cry unable to cut itself off   of the same dust that now weighs down the dark

the breath that chases space before you this inward step that measures you and carves you out

may he enflame me with the kisses of his mouth!

ḤAMSĪN

transparent hell of Arābāh
we've been walking forever
in the vitreous flaming body of God
columns of sand and sheaves of the wind
strides in the sphere of the poor
we've been walking forever
in a crumbly wall of granite
in the whistling of the fire that rises
from the earth damasked in the pink of the lungs

we've been walking forever

on the dreaming waters of the world

How many paths have we not traced in the nakedness of our bodies!
How many crests, how many dividing lines carried until collapse!
Into this country of no path let him from no place come. Let the light that fells us come. We are trembling just enough to keep our thirst intact.

EARTH ABSOLUTE

I seek the dagger of the trail in this noon hoarse with shouting
I seek a covert wing in my opaque and heavy step
a singing possible for my tongue stuck to the dust
a lip more than memory for my parched lips
I seek a breath at the bottom of the stones
a coolness that rises in the cistern of the eyes
final water where the light kneels down.
I await the night with its scorpions.
With the precise star at the hour of falling silent.
And it was necessary to undress time after time
to empty   to excavate   to exfoliate the self.
O imprudent traveler!
So you did not suspect the dark cave of your eye
o too careful gaze!

Holocaust by fire, fragrance soothing for the pleura of the evening slipping down low on the porous hilltops.

Rough God of a hard land, of an earth injurious to every ornamented thing.

God without name in this land without place, scent of stone from our abandoned camps.

Your book, your word, your eruptions of lava and pitch are silenced.

Silenced against the light that's sulking in the rocks, appearing in the pores and pollens of the cooled volcano.

The balms of Jericho are soothing the razed slopes, the sky muted of birds.

The surveyor folds up his markers, his cards, his cross-staff and leveling rods, his trapezoids & triangles to listen suddenly.

To listen to the beat of the transparent body of his eye in the creaking of the chalks.

Vacant your heaviness. The song bursts out in the density of the world reenclosed.

You don't ask: "Where are you? who?"

Your mouth is rough, your tongue lamed in the seamless face.

EARTH ABSOLUTE

Far beneath my step trembles my step
Far beneath this path trembles the path
from having struck the indisputable harshness
and the eye that comes to meet the eye
and here beneath the eyelashes the liquefied mountain.

*This great body of beige mineral
which a thousand cubits down
decays in the water of its death.
And lower still
where you can't distinguish heights any longer
this peerless disaster stripping you.*

DESERT WATERS

When you undertake to leap-frog down the rounded mountains in the desert of Judea, toward the bottom of the

       great   tectonic   fault,

arriving at the base, devoured by thirst, you will perceive a great expanse of water

       WATER

No, it isn't a mirage.

       Vast surface of water
       of a dark blue
       bordering on indigo
       cut like a precious gem
       in the brown ocher of the
       Mountains of Moab.

You'll need to taste the stench of bitumen and the acrid bite of potassium salts to understand that this body of water isn't made for quenching thirst. It is the

FETID LAKE

Tons of arid and malodorous water

> Aristotle remarks: "If there really exists in Palestine, as we are told, a lake such that if a man or a beast of burden is plunged therein, with its limbs tied, the body floats and does not sink to the bottom, then this would be a confirmation of what we were just saying (that salt water is heavier than fresh water), for we are assured the water in this lake is so bitter and so salty that no fish can live in it and that it suffices, to clean clothes, to immerse them in it and then shake them out."

(Let us note this last assertion has not received experimental verification in our time.)

> Aristotle thought that fish died in this water from being unable to *sink down in it*. It was Galen of Pergamum who first put forward the idea that it must be *the excessive bitterness that proved fatal to living beings.*

Since then, we have learned that life does not recoil from any bitterness. In this revolting brine (made up of sodium chlorate, manganese, calcium, potassium and certain bromides), algae of the species *Dunaliella* adjust their osmotic pressure by producing glycerol; several species of bacteria grow there on good terms. Some anærobes of the genus *Clostridium* explain the formation in deep anoxic water of iron sulphide, well-known for its smell of rotten eggs.

> Flavius Josephus recounts that Vespasian, to lend experimental verification to assertions that the heaviest bodies thrown in there became so light it was impossible to submerge them, ordered that people who could not swim, whose hands were tied behind their back, be thrown offshore. *Now, all of them floated as if buoyed by the spirit.*

If the effects of salinity intrigued thinkers, the stench & the miasma filled them with all kinds of anxiety.

> The Arab geographer Yāqūt writes toward 1225: "The fetid odor of the lake is extremely

> noxious and in certain years the miasma spreads throughout the land and causes the death of every living creature."

and Tacitus:
> "I am willing to admit that formerly celebrated cities were burned by fire from the heavens, but I consider that miasmas from the lake infect the earth, corrupt the air in which it bathes, and subsequently cause the autumn fruits to rot, the soil being equally unhealthy."

The extraction of bitumen from the Dead Sea, called *Lake Asphaltites* by the Ancients, was undoubtedly the principal source of wealth in the environs of Sodom. Used as construction materials and caulking for small boats, it was much sought-after by the
e m b a l m e r s
of Egypt.

> Strabo describes in his treatise on geography the asphalt emissions from the lake of Sodom:
>
> "In indeterminate eras,
> *this substance springs from the middle of the abyss*

> with bubbles like those of boiling water; its external surface gives it the look of a hill. It is accompanied by abundant soot that takes the form of smoke though imperceptible to the eye, which nonetheless tarnishes all shiny metal... It is in fact in seeing their utensils tarnish that river-dwellers are forewarned of an imminent eruption of bitumen; they then prepare themselves to harvest it on rafts woven of reeds..."

According to Posidonius, the people of the country, who are sorcerers, have a procedure which gives to asphalt a consistency allowing it to be cut in pieces:
they pronounce certain magical incantations, simultaneously permeating the asphalt with urine and other malodorous liquids.

> Perhaps it is urine itself that has this solidifying property, as when it forms stones in the bladder or chrysocolla is prepared from a child's urine.

The author of the RHIND papyrus, in direct address to the deceased, writes:

"Anubis, as taricheute,
fill your cavities with mnnyny"

> This mnnyny is probably analogous to the m u m y ā , or m u m m y of Arab & Greek authors. It designates a mineral substance that is

BLACK

most probably identical to

BITUMEN

PISSASPHALT

that is mumyā after it is carried down by the waters of the high mountains. It takes its definitive form when it arrives at the end of its run:

"... then, thickened and having
a sticky appearance, it gives off
an odor of pitch mixed with
asphalt,"

> says Ibn Al-Baitar, in his *Treatise on the Simple.*

the

RITUAL OF EMBALMING

speaks of an ointment called

"Salve of stone that blackens the phallus"

it also revives the use of the legs and hearing.

"The mummy of the tombs"

> found in Arab authors probably corresponds to a product composed of
> > pissasphalt
> > various aromatic herbs
> > & precious porphyritic
> > stones.
>
> In the 18th century huge quantities were shipped to Europe. It is said to be excellent for contusions and certain conditions of circulation and respiration.

Ambroise Paré reports that in the store of a Jew in Alexandria, one of the King of Navarre's doctors came upon forty or so bodies crudely embalmed by the merchant. These embalmed bodies, from which "momie" could be extracted, were sold for medical use. *The cadavers whose viscera were removed were dried out in an oven, then soaked in black pitch.*

> The opposite of black mummy obtained in this way was white mummy produced by

THE CADAVERS OF TRAVELERS WHO DIED IN THE DESERT

If you are lucky enough to be able to acquire a little white or black mummy you will be able to use it effectively against

> pituitary or algid cephalalgy
> migraines
> paralysis
> facial tics
> epilepsy
> vertigo

if you dissolve some the size of a grain in jasmine oil you will obtain a powerful remedy for

> earaches

it is necessary to dissolve a q u i r a t e in mulberry syrup or in a decoction of lentils and licorice for

> palpitations

and a grain mixed with the decoction of wild celery and cumin from Kerman for

> hiccups.

And all the same
> in the burning groin of the South
great blue sharks and butterflies come to frolic
> between the mineral mink and limestone of deer
> between the mountains of iron which lay bare
the eye and the iridescent winds of a beginning
here where God spoke to his peoples
> between the black lavas of Sinaï
> and the tan brasier of Djebel Hirā
> between Him who walked into the fire
> and Him who came across
> patches of caved-in sky
He who formed man out of clay and
He who created him out of coagulated blood
> there is the song of the sea
> there is this great supple body of lilacs
> and the eighteen poison arrows underneath the
> ruffled feathers of the flying pterois

RED SEA
> with flesh the purple of the desert iris
> with entrails of sepia coral
> and farther down
>> in the deep mines of the night
>> a final flame
>> of coral fire.

And once more
>   having left behind that first fault
>   orange and green
which hatches under the nocturnal vault of steel
>   we walked in this hard land
>   of thirst and dreams,
walked from the abrupt brow to the softer flanks
>   of the light,
wandering from how faraway?
and what distances traversed without ever
>   ever having left
>   the close center of silence?

EARTH ABSOLUTE

Here
    all the earth
           rests from its fertility
and all its happiness is stretched between
        two gazelles and two nights
scarcely distant from a fold in the light
        and the tranquil challenge
of the impregnable horizon.

Look at me one more time
Unshadowed blood relative racing the sun —
in this hollow where our viscera slowly erode
these paths of lymph misting the evening
our rivers where the memory of fire is setting.

You grow silent once again.
You hear the echo
of the beaten path sink back.
Defeated like a flight deprived of air
and the fall stripped of its center of gravity.
No listening, no track, no trace.

Jerusalem, 1954–1970.

ENDNOTES TO EARTH ABSOLUTE

Page 102   Job 6:15. Author's adaptation.

Page 103   Ḥārra: expanse covered with volcanic rock, such as one often encounters in Arabia. Ḥamd: praise. Hegira: emigration, its archetypcal use to designate the Emigration of Mohammed from Mecca to Medina.

Page 111   Exodus 4:25.

Page 119   Royal caves (βασιλικά σπήλαια), a name given by Josephus to the hard limestone quarries called Malaki (royal) in Jerusalem.

Page 119   I Kings 5:31.

Page 119   Leviticus 14:34.

Page 121   The word desert in Sumerian: *edin* (or in Akkadian: *ṣēru*); in Hebrew: m d b r ; in Ugaritic: m d b r ; in Egyptian (hieroglyph); and in Arabic: *Saḥra*.

Page 139   Poem by the author, translated into Arabic by S. El Joundi.

Page 142   Hosea 2:16.

Page 144   Hosea 2:4. Author's adaptation.

Page 146   After Zimmern, *Tammuzlieder*; Myhormann, *Babylonian Hymns and Prayers*; Reisner, *Hymnen*, № 8. Author's adaptation.

Page 150   Cf. J. B. Pritchard, *Ancient Near Eastern Texts Relating to the Old Testament*; R. de Vaux, *Histoire ancienne* d'Israel; J. R. Kupper, *Les Nomades en Mesopotamie au temps des rois de Mari*.

Page 159 Badiet et Tīh, a desert on the Sinai Peninsula.

Page 164 Psalms 106:13–14.

Page 165 *Histoire des moines d'Egypte* by Rufin d'Aquilée.

Page 165 *Vie de Sainte Marie l'Egyptienne*; texts cited by Jacques Lacarrière in *Les Hommes ivres de Dieu*.

Page 166 *Life of Macaire*, Coptic text.

Page 166 Jean Climaque, *Echelle*, degree 27, cited by Lacarrière.

Page 168 Rufin, *Histoire des moines d'Egypte*.

Page 170 Isaiah 34:14–15.

Page 178 Ezekiel 27:21.

Page 180 *Tranquilles sont les espions*, translated by G. Makdisi and J. Grosjean.

Page 183 Genesis 31:40.

Page 185 "Chanfara." Translation by S. de Sacy. The final paragraph was inspired by a Bedouin poem (oral tradition).

Page 188 Ḥamsīn, the name given, in the Near East, to the hot wind from the south, laden with sand.

Page 197 The rerouting of the waters of the Jordan for the benefit of agriculture has, over the course of the past few years, significantly lowered the level of the Dead Sea (by around 6 meters in 1979). Evaporation exceeding replenishment of fresh water, an increase has occurred in the salinity of the upper layers (30–50 meters), until now isolated by the gradient of salinity from the inert, much denser depths. The reduced difference in density between the two layers has at last unleashed circulatory movements destroying stratification & leading to an equalization of salinity. All this, of course, has been accompanied by a significant diminution in the number of micro-organisms.

Corrosive Body

She would come in the evening's hollow
dispersing the paths
would come unclothed of distances
would come from the non-country
would come bare tune in her flesh
never pronounced.

Two words run in our veins, clasp and unclasp
the blossoming of buds.
Tree and lightning of the same space
of the same pulse unfolded red in the wind.

A rose so pale hoisted itself up in the sun.
The wheat continues to stir
behind our pupils
                as if space were gently
    crying for help.

In summer when the pomegranates split open and rot
    the wells
between the crickets smashed by the bull-dozers
the earth held up by
long transfusions of nights.

Our hands still discover
under the solar uproar
the silent snake.

In the almond of the cry that was never opened
the weight too dense for the name,
a sowing set down in the estuary of our tongues.
In the vulva night
melted in pleasure
the work of breath and of blood.
Witnesses surely, but how to come back
when the shores of the path shatter
the song shatters in the fire.

Upon the ardent threshold
rebellious pilgrim
I set my insomnia down.
We precede the day
with a length of light.

Heaven without beams and without mast
light maddened by murderous blues
and beiges, beiges and downy
bronzes of the slopes where fingers shout
and you don't understand.

CORROSIVE BODY

Birds that precede the light in your throats
prepare the path of the blind.
Crossing through the anfractuous rock
with a thin blade of quivering flesh
you break our mirrors still today.

Word clasped under the teguments of black,
at the ebb of the springs.
Path of affluence
where she never came, never went.
Under the porch where the barbarian is welcomed
amid the fire, the arrows and death
I have laid the steppes on your stomach
and with burned tongue I listened
to the deep throb of your waters.

Summer of paths, of dust. Earth without membrane
    or lungs.
The slight water of the halt
drunk at the mouths of another burned body.
Under a great tree's sleep wandering frees us
to a darker flame
without compass and without rod.

Incoercible hollowing,
dehiscent touch of carnal gravity
you steal me from my weight.

The sewer of chatty words and their lymph
drained from the rivers of muteness.
On the murderous path, in wild loneness,
you listened to sweetness coming
to drink in this infected water.
Your peaceful shouting of the great depths
when the knife of light falls.

Slowness of our members making their way
between the iron and sensuousness.
The same face going toward its absence of face
bringing its threatened freshness, its tepid night
to this bare sojourn.

You so white, sumptuous severity
compact whirlwind slowly unpinned,
without renouncing your first rigor,
incisive prescription,
Open Heart of the Rule.

Muscular lock where motion heats up
standing on the sill enlivened
the oceanic door opened
on our softly eroded hinges

On the steps of the dawn
our beds where jellyfish are drying.

CORROSIVE BODY

Under the bond of the sun
the tender affair of pulverized hands.
The sand drinks us at the groin of our resurgences.

We were diving far out from the Sporades of memory,
distant from the cries and the drums of a bygone time.
From the thistles, a shipwrecked chapel of blue.

We were asking the salt to break through the shell
asking the waters to pursue our bare slopes.
Under our fingers the same translucent crabs were running
deepening the sands by the same blue point
and with one mouth we were drinking
the growing darkness in long drafts.

Sweetness of the shadows ambushed under the loins
drawn by the ten pencils of the groping.
The barbaric rush curved by the hip,
narrowed by the arches, and our hands slowly
laid down in the garden floats of the sea.

Votive cysts on the abyss of calm.
Night of space, here are our markings!
You can put down your greedy madness
in our lapidary brevity —
pause and recognize your dispersed bronze

its wild corn of the antipodes where
the light tries to catch its breath.
Kneaded on your wharves, the smoking density of our
    sensuousness.
Frozen animals rub against them in the winter.

In this place language is so dense
that the flesh leans over
and we miss something in the support
like the sudden lack of the wing turning toward space —
you know, you have seen predictions,
you want to cry out
and there's no sound.

Blind cry of the white of the eye
against the white
of the walls.
I love you devastating season, matrix broken with heat,
your fires blued with winds, your liquid distances
drying upon my skin.
I love your thirst and your rigorous oblivion
stabbing the conqueror.

I'm always seeking the same blind evening
whose earth eaten by solar acids
ferments in its flesh of such heated browns
that the eyes tremble in the pulse becalmed.

Chalk path issuing from the dark hollow
climbing straight up and rethinking space
irrigated by your center of redness
pardon the sky the death of the day and of the god —
invent ceaselessly, tiring yourself,
the simple, the paltry, the nothing.

Summer's end.
Your hips of Judea, of Moab, of Edom
explored, engraved with fevers and with saffron.
Now that the sky discovers its shadows
they reveal their weapons of brightness.
Under the increasing weight of the evening
The ravished corn of the embrace.

Your sun still burns
sun of darts, poisons —
here the summer is ruined.
The silent mercury of our body to body
spurts in the door of the day,
roaming mast of the enclosure of light:
here there sank the figurehead.

For under the intractable harshness
when the sun beats us down face to earth
under our motions of agony and of joy
we find once more the floats in the sea.

Stripped of reflections, the riot has drilled its well.
Under the clouding of the day
— what forces doesn't it use to convince us —
we had to find again this simple bed
the ravine where the migrating bird is broken.

Ah, how this day was surely sliding between our cyclamen walls!
Is dissolving.
And the cavern gorged with nights with its coral imperatives!
Sun o white weapon upon the sands
the sea plunges us in an unknown breast.
Perhaps our hands see more clearly
in the dusk where so many beginnings of so much childhood
move about.
From the towpaths younger than the age of who sees
where we are coming endlessly shining in the dark.

For an arduous science of our darks:
The silence, the thunder, the artery.
The bird force, a calm ember,
Fascinates the inks of the stormy weather,
word of morning in the throats of heaviness
it holds dispersion on a leash.
Let the flakes of time fall,
let our bodies snow —

CORROSIVE BODY

In the bony arena the opulence of loins.
On high the seagulls interlace their cries
when the blue hegira uproots them from the sea.
In the palm of the shadow the bivalve of the setting sun
the soul's mother-of-pearl in the stressed flesh —
the wreck brighter than the work.
Here we lay down our names.
Thirst spilled forth in the silt of river mouths,
voracious fish in the splendor of fruits.
The oyster by slowness, exhaustions
designs the grey nerves of its dreams.
Sewn with the rhythms of undertow and arteries
our putrescent weathers magnificently sing!

Fortunate dispersion!
Fatal trace of the eye!
Our whispered bloods dance over there
upon the peaks of mists.
We have dug in the wave under its thorns
tracked some famous sunsets and have been
snakes in the fountain of our gestures.

Our words make night in the dazzle,
in our veins bluer than the evening
the sun replants its secret oranges,
its daggers of the west.
Music where the sweet dark wound opened,
a new halt in the god's eloquence.

Here circled
with black and with furtive abysses
struggled the mast of blood and the inherited sea swell.
At dawn: a little water trembling
in the navel of a stone.

Musical curve a lamp inside easily composes,
the valley of the song brightens the celebrant's bulk.
The opaque flesh lit by the flesh
opens its ravines in the certainty of grasp.
Convent of Cyclades in the abrupt night —
our chalk weeps a long time in the cliff.

Under the sleeping foliage of fire
the mouth to love, to insult.
O the fervent work in the black cavern of colors!
And the muteness all around,
the conspiracy of nights
and the age-old recitation eroding the dancer.

Song in the muscles of the song —
jubilation of pulp in the solar millstone!
We gaily cast our words into the fire,
the embers will sleep with our insomnias.
The hot nerves of sleep
will dream to the very end of the cold.

Here, this angle, this our home, cleared in the incurable
 infinite,
our camp at the edge of centuries far out from our souls
under our tents the bright-dark whisper of blood
coming near with its corals, its stalks,
its blind ones.
In the eyes wide open slowly the world consumes itself,
our hands upon the earth open and wither.

Evening, nothing.
However the black constructs itself, circumspect, careful.
From near to near, proceeding by gangrene in the massive
 clarity,
by hemorrhaging.
Walls and hills beaten down
daring presences in the distancing.
Elsewhere
a chilly underneath of foliage,
soundless
rooms placed right at the waiting.
Patience. Crystals of patience. Lights & shattered gestures.
Lagunas of air on the loins, under the hand that curves
 them,
tread of the distance on the familiar threshold, unfolding
 its valves,
its leavings, its tumults
and you are seeking how the light breathes
in so much dark groping.

The sun rots under the skin.
The shadows are from the south and the depths
of the sky rust at the edge of our members.
Our mouths full of myrtles
burst apart between the sea columns.
She would come in the evening's hollow
dispersing the paths
would come unclothed of distances
would come from the non-country
would come bare tune in her flesh
never pronounced.

Jerusalem 1970, Patmos 1975

Bibliography

WORKS BY LORAND GASPAR

Poetry

Le quatrième etat de la matière (Paris: Flammarion, 1966).
Gisements (Paris: Flammarion, 1968).
Sol absolu (Paris: Gallimard, 1972).
Corps corrosifs (Paris: Fata Morgana, 1978).
Egée, suivi de Judée (Paris: Gallimard, 1980).
Sol absolu et autres textes (Paris: Gallimard, 1982).
Feuilles d'observation et de La Maison près de la mer (Paris: Poésie / Gallimard, 1993).
Patmos et autres poèmes (Paris: Gallimard, 2001).

Prose

Approche de la Parole (Paris: Gallimard, 1978). Réédition augmentée d'Apprentissage (Paris: Gallimard, 2004).
Journaux de Voyage (Paris: Picquier-Le Calligraphe, 1985).
Feuilles d'Observation (Paris: Gallimard, 1986).
Carnet de Patmos (Bazas: Le Temps qu'il fait, 1991).
Arabie heureuse, réédition revue et corrigée, de journaux de voyage, augmenté de trois nouveaux récits (Paris: Deyrolle, 1997).
Carnets de Jérusalem (Bazas: Le temps qu'il fait, 1997).
Essai: Histoire de la Palestine (Paris: Maspero, 1968).
    Edition revue et augmentée, 1978.

Photography

Mouvementé de mots et de couleurs: photographies de l'auteur, textes de James Sacré (Bazas: Le temps qu'il fait, 2003).

Critical Sources on Lorand Gaspar

Cahiers Lorand Gaspar (Le temps qu'il fait: avril 2004).
Europe (October 2005). Special issue on Lorand Gaspar.
Glenn Fetzer, "Lorand Gaspar: Poésie à la rencontre des sciences neurocognitives," *French Forum* Vol. 38, Nºs 1–2 (2013).

———. "Lorand Gaspar et la parole arborescente."

———. "Interroger la langue, dépister la maladie: écriture et médecine chez Lorand Gaspar," *Lublin Studies in Modern Languages and Literature* 38, Nº 1 (2014). www.lsmll.umcs.lublin.pl

Jérôme Hennebert, "Le livre de poésie et son morcellement: *Sol absolu* de Lorand Gaspar," *Le livre et ses espaces* (Presses universitaires de Paris Ouest: Open Edition Books, 2007). http://books.openedition.org.

Daniela Hurezanu *&* Stephen Kessler, "Between Poetic Vision and Scientific Knowledge: Lorand Gaspar," Translator's Note to Lorand Gaspar's "Poem" from *Nights* (Cerise Press, 2007).

Laurent Margantin, "Respiration de flûte dans le poids du calcaire. Entretien Lorand Gaspar / Laurent Margantin." http://remue.net/revue/TXT0310_MargGasp.html.

———. "Rainer Maria Rilke, Lorand Gaspar et 'l'autre rapport'." www.oeuvresouvertes.net/spip.php?article104.

Marina Ondo, "Lorand Gaspar, faire la lumière sur l'origine du secret." www.larevuedesressources.org/lorand-gaspar-faire-la-lumiere-sur-l'origine-du-secret,1336.html (20 décembre 2013).

COLOPHON

EARTH ABSOLUTE

was typeset in InDesign CC.

The text & page numbers are set in *Adobe Jenson Pro*.
The titles are set in *Escritura*.

Book design & typesetting: Alessandro Segalini
Cover design: Contra Mundum Press

EARTH ABSOLUTE

is published by Contra Mundum Press.
Its printer has received Chain of Custody certification from:
The Forest Stewardship Council,
The Programme for the Endorsement of Forest Certification,
& The Sustainable Forestry Initiative.

Contra Mundum Press   New York · London · Melbourne

CONTRA MUNDUM PRESS

Dedicated to the value & the indispensable importance of the individual voice, to works that test the boundaries of thought & experience.

The primary aim of Contra Mundum is to publish translations of writers who in their use of form and style are *à rebours*, or who deviate significantly from more programmatic & spurious forms of experimentation. Such writing attests to the volatile nature of modernism. Our preference is for works that have not yet been translated into English, are out of print, or are poorly translated, for writers whose thinking & æsthetics are in opposition to timely or mainstream currents of thought, value systems, or moralities. We also reprint obscure and out-of-print works we consider significant but which have been forgotten, neglected, or overshadowed.

There are many works of fundamental significance to *Weltliteratur* (& *Weltkultur*) that still remain in relative oblivion, works that alter and disrupt standard circuits of thought — these warrant being encountered by the world at large. It is our aim to render them more visible.

For the complete list of forthcoming publications, please visit our website. To be added to our mailing list, send your name and email address to: info@contramundum.net

Contra Mundum Press
P.O. Box 1326
New York, NY 10276
USA

OTHER CONTRA MUNDUM PRESS TITLES

Gilgamesh
Ghérasim Luca, *Self-Shadowing Prey*
Rainer J. Hanshe, *The Abdication*
Walter Jackson Bate, *Negative Capability*
Miklós Szentkuthy, *Marginalia on Casanova*
Fernando Pessoa, *Philosophical Essays*
Elio Petri, *Writings on Cinema & Life*
Friedrich Nietzsche, *The Greek Music Drama*
Richard Foreman, *Plays with Films*
Louis-Auguste Blanqui, *Eternity by the Stars*
Miklós Szentkuthy, *Towards the One & Only Metaphor*
Josef Winkler, *When the Time Comes*
William Wordsworth, *Fragments*
Josef Winkler, *Natura Morta*
Fernando Pessoa, *The Transformation Book*
Emilio Villa, *The Selected Poetry of Emilio Villa*
Robert Kelly, *A Voice Full of Cities*
Pier Paolo Pasolini, *The Divine Mimesis*
Miklós Szentkuthy, *Prae, Vol. 1*
Federico Fellini, *Making a Film*
Robert Musil, *Thought Flights*
Sándor Tar, *Our Street*

SOME FORTHCOMING TITLES

Jean-Luc Godard, *Phrases*
Pierre Senges, *The Major Refutation*

About the Translators

Mary Ann Caws is Distinguished Professor of English, French, & Comparative Literature at the Graduate Center of the City University of New York, the recipient of Guggenheim, Rockefeller, and Fulbright fellowships, a fellow of the American Academy of Arts and Sciences, the past president of the Modern Language Association & the American Comparative Literature Association. She is the author of *Surprised in Translation*, the *Modern Art Cookbook*, of many books on art and text, including critical lives of Picasso, Dali, Henry James, Marcel Proust, Virginia Woolf, Vita Sackville-West, and Blaise Pascal, volumes of translation of Mallarmé, Tzara, Breton, Char, and Reverdy among others, and the editor of the *Yale Anthology of French Twentieth-Century Poetry*.

Nancy Kline has published nine books, including a novel, a critical study of René Char's poetry, a biography of Elizabeth Blackwell, and translations of Char, Paul Éluard, Jules Supervielle, and other modern French writers. Kline's short stories, essays, memoirs and flash nonfictions have appeared widely. She reviews for the *New York Times Sunday Book Review* and has received a National Endowment for the Arts Creative Writing Grant. For many years she taught at Barnard College of Columbia University, as Founding Director of the Barnard Writing Program. She now teaches for Poets & Writers and the Bard Prison Initiative, and is an Associate of the Bard Institute for Writing & Thinking. She is currently completing a book of creative nonfiction entitled *Other Geographies* and a memoir entitled *Hunger and Return*.

www.ingramcontent.com/pod-product-compliance
Lightning Source LLC
Chambersburg PA
CBHW071111160426
43196CB00013B/2538